Collins Wide World Encyclopedias

The Animal Kingdom

Compiled and edited by Kenneth Bailey

AF593817

Collins

Glasgow and London

Written by Alfred Leutscher, Joyce Pope
Designed by Peter Sullivan, Charles Gould

Illustrated by E. Crosby-Smith, The Garden Studio, Charles Gould, John Grimwade, David Johnson, Anthony Joyce, Peter McGinn, Duncan Mil, David Nash, Edward Osmond, David Pratt, John Rignell, George Thompson, Maurice Wilson, Michael Woods

First published in this edition 1976
Second impression 1977
Published by William Collins Sons and Company Limited, Glasgow and London

© 1973, 1976 William Collins Sons and Company Limited
Printed in Great Britain
ISBN 0 00 106302 2

Contents

Animals with Backbones

Although the vast majority of creatures in the world belong to the group called invertebrates, that is animals without backbones, it is the vertebrates, or animals with backbones, that command our principal interest. This is understandable because vertebrates include not only man himself but all the more familiar animals, such as lions and tigers, cats and dogs.

For most of us it is difficult enough to think of fishes or frogs as animals, let alone cockroaches or one-celled protozoans. But the fact remains that the animal kingdom is made up of many groups (called phyla) of invertebrates and only one group of vertebrates. However dissimilar fishes, amphibians, reptiles, birds and mammals may seem, they have much more in common with one another than with any of the invertebrates.

The vertebrates, and mammals in particular, clearly represent the highest form of development in the animal kingdom. This has to do chiefly with greater brain power, which has led to man's superior position in the world today, not only over other mammals but over all creatures.

Living in Water

Although the first vertebrates came into being more than 600 million years ago they all lived in water until about 350 million years ago. Even today, all vertebrates at some stage in their development have openings or slits at the side of the throat forming a passage from the exterior to the pharynx, which is the upper part of the passage in the neck through which food is taken. In land mammals, reptiles and birds these slits are present only in the very early stages of the animal embryo. They perform no function, merely indicating that the ancestors of these creatures once had need of them in order to breathe. In fish, they continue to exist as gill-slits.

The true vertebrates consist of a series of classes—fishes, amphibians, reptiles, birds and mammals—which represent successive evolutionary steps from lower to higher orders of animals much more clearly than any links which can be traced between the various groups of invertebrates.

Vertebrates take their name from the vertebral column, or backbone, which all members of the group possess. In the skeleton of an animal the backbone is the jointed rod which extends from the back of the head to the base of the body or, when present, to the tip of the tail.

Within the vertebral column and protected by it, is the spinal cord which connects with the brain. The brain is the chief part of the nervous system, and the organs of sensation, such as the spinal cord, are really outgrowths from it. This arrangement whereby the nervous system is enclosed within a bony tube separate from the rest of the body is peculiar to the vertebrates. The nervous system in invertebrates is enclosed within the general body cavity ánd is not in any way shut off.

The Vertebral Column

The vertebral column consists of a succession of bony segments each joined to its neighbour in such a way that the animal may flex its body. The segments, or joints, of which the backbone is composed are usually formed of bone in adult animals. Some of the more primitive vertebrates, such as sharks and rays among the fishes, may retain the pliable material, called cartilage, of which the skeleton is first formed and never develop proper bones.

Two other important characteristics of vertebrates are the limbs, which are present in most species and never exceed four in number, and the jaws, which are upper and lower rather than right and left as in insects.

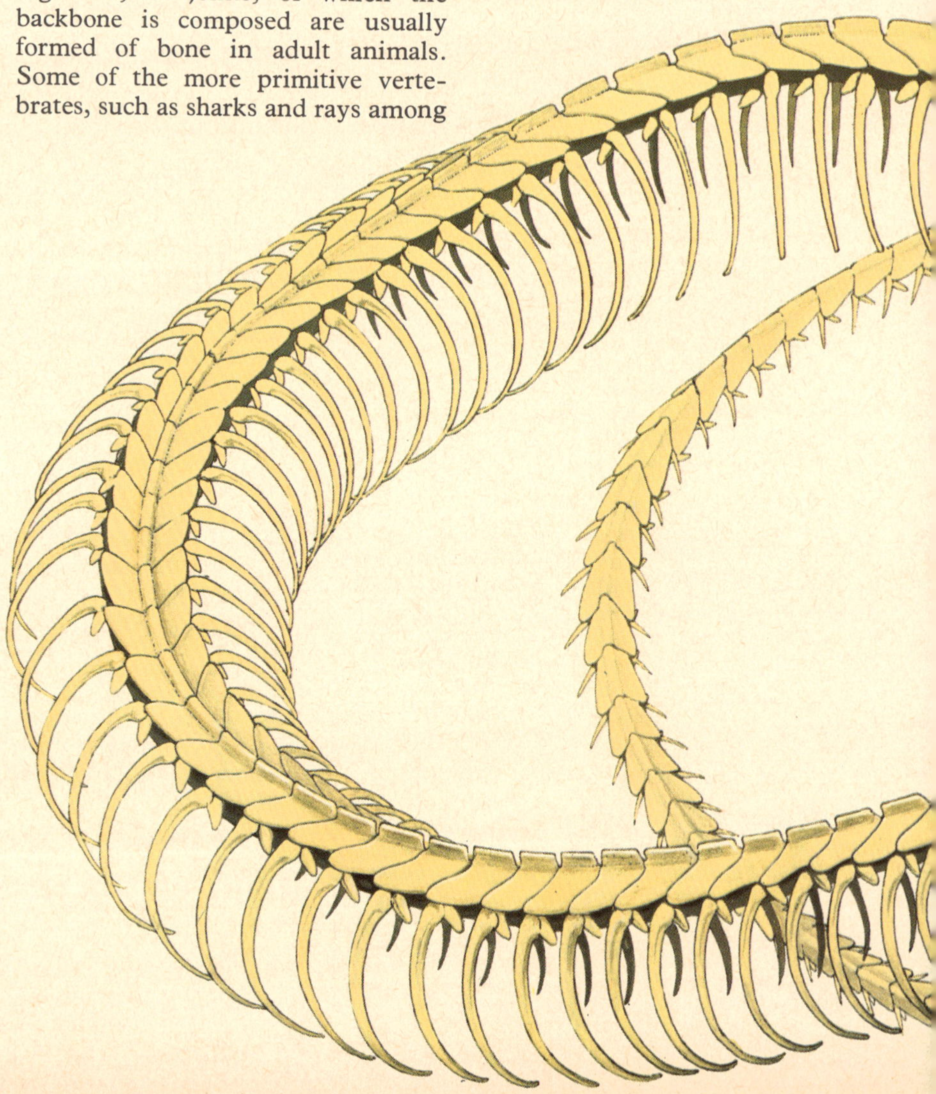

Primitive Chordates

Allied with the vertebrates within the major group called chordates, are a number of very primitive creatures which, although they have no vertebrae, are like the backboned animals in many important ways. They live in or near the sea, the most numerous being the sea-squirts, of which there are no less than 1,200 species.

The Five Classes

Vertebrate animals are divided into five classes and each of these will be looked at in greater detail on the succeeding pages. They are presented in their evolutionary order, beginning with fishes and ending with man.

1. Fishes (scientific name Pisces, from the Latin *piscis*, a fish). Living in water; cold-blooded; mostly breathing through gills; three groups.
2. Amphibians (scientific name Amphibia, from the Greek *amphibios*, having a double life). Fish-like in their early existence; breathing through gills at first, then acquiring lungs; three groups.
3. Reptiles (scientific name Reptilia, from the Latin *repere*, to creep). Bony skeletons; skin clothed with horny plates or scales; most lay eggs but some produce live young; four groups.
4. Birds (scientific name Aves, from the Latin *avis*, a bird). Feathered; warm-blooded; young hatched from eggs; forelimbs developed into wings used in flight; twenty-seven groups.
5. Mammals (scientific name Mammalia, from the Latin *mamma*, the breast). Warm-blooded; producing live young; skin covered usually with hair; breathing air by lungs; young suckled on milk from mother; three groups, egg-laying, marsupial and placental.

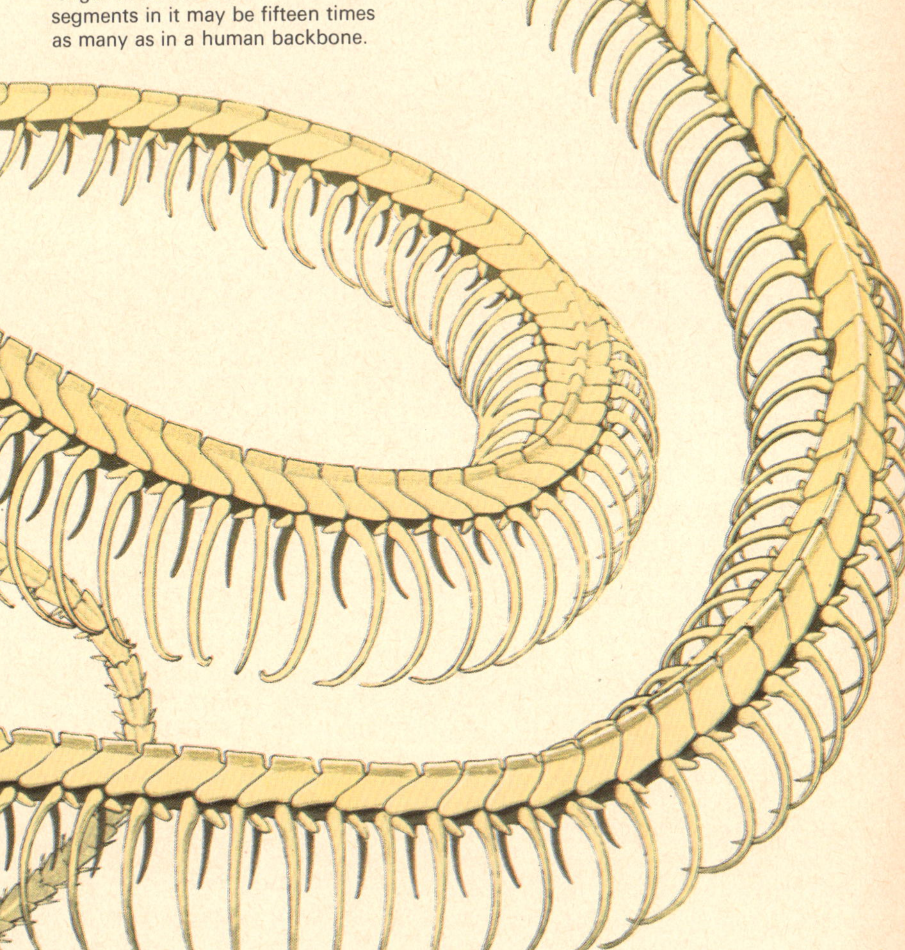

The skeleton ot a snake shows the length of its backbone. The number of segments in it may be fifteen times as many as in a human backbone.

Fishes

Bony Fishes

The great majority of fishes existing in the world today fall into this class. They are distinguished from the cartilaginous fishes by the bony nature of their skeletons. The structure of the skeleton is important as a guide to the classification of the different kinds of fishes.

The sturgeon and its allies form a sub-class of bony fishes separate from all others. They are slow-moving, often heavy fish, some living in the open sea and going up river to spawn, and others spending all their lives in rivers. They are characterised by numbers of bony plates on their sides and a long bony snout with which they root about in the mud of river beds looking for food.

Herring shoals can stretch for several kilometres. The fish are usually caught in drift nets, which are like huge curtains hung from buoys floating on the surface of the water.

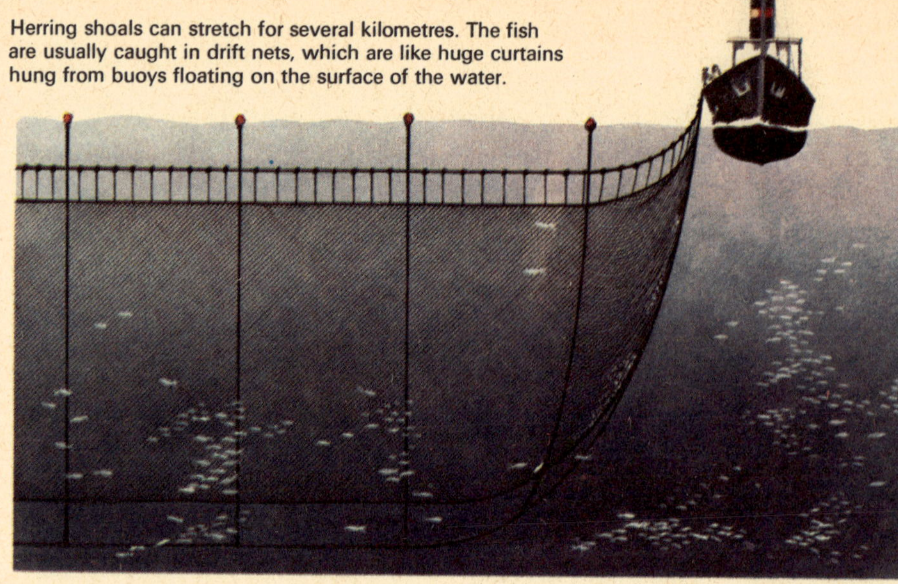

The typical sturgeons are confined to northern waters of temperate regions, where they are among the largest of freshwater fishes. Some specimens have been known over six metres (twenty feet) in length but the average size is much smaller. The sturgeon used to be important economically, particularly in Europe, before its numbers dropped. Its flesh was regarded as a delicacy, its eggs provided caviare, the lining of its swim bladder was used for making glue, and a grained fish leather was made from its skin. In Britain it has been a 'royal' fish since the reign of Edward II (1307–27), by whose act it was proclaimed that all sturgeon caught off the coasts of the kingdom should belong to the sovereign.

It is said of sturgeon that in winter they go into some form of hibernation. Stories from some localities tell of them burying their noses in the mud with bodies and tails standing straight upright like a series of posts.

Other members of this group include paddlefishes, birchirs and reedfishes.

Common sturgeon

Herrings

The herring is the most important food fish in the world. It is eaten fresh, salted or potted and, smoked and slit apart, it becomes that popular dish the kipper. It lives in the temperate seas of the northern hemisphere, particularly in the North Atlantic. Millions of them swim together in vast shoals near the surface of the water. For generations a complete industry has existed around their capture and marketing, particularly in Great Britain, France and the Scandinavian countries.

The herring has a strong claim to be the most numerous backboned animal in existence and thousands of millions of them are caught every year. Also popular and abundant as food fishes are sprats, whitebait (which are in fact the young of herrings and sprats), pilchards (and their young, sardines) and anchovies. The sardine has only feeble bones and is usually eaten whole. The largest shoals of them are found around the island of Sardinia, hence their name.

This skeleton of a perch illustrates the structure of a typical bony fish.

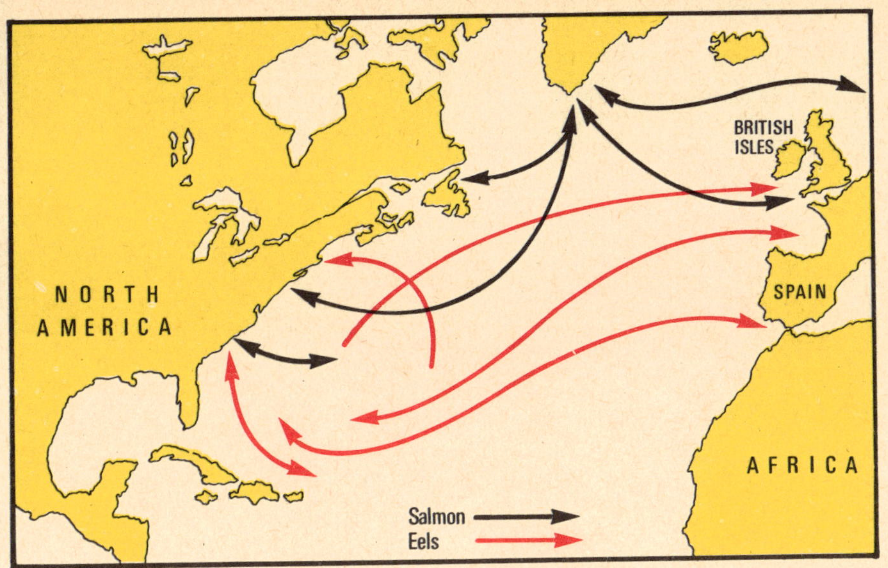

The map illustrates the general direction of the routes taken by salmon and eels on their migratory journeys across the Atlantic Ocean. The eel moves from rivers to the sea to spawn and the salmon does the same thing in reverse.

The common eel is widely distributed in fresh waters throughout the world.

Eels

The typical adult eel is long and snake-like in appearance. The majority of species live in the sea but the members of one family, the Anguillidae, spend their adult lives in rivers. The most familiar example is the common European eel, which is widely distributed all over the continent.

The eel's extraordinary life-history follows a regular pattern. It grows slowly and lives in the fresh water of rivers for an average of eight to ten years, although the males stay longer than the females. Each autumn a great number of eels decide to leave the rivers to breed.

During their journey into the Atlantic Ocean they do not eat, having stored up large food reserves in their bodies. After several months the eels arrive at an area in the Atlantic near the Sargasso Sea and here they spawn and afterwards die, for no adult eels are known to have returned to their river homes. The young larvae then develop in the depths of the oceans and begin their long, slow trek back to the rivers. This takes them about three years, during which time they are tiny transparent beings. When they arrive in coastal waters off Europe they have grown to about 70 millimetres (three inches) in length and as they make for the rivers they gradually assume a cylindrical shape, become elvers, or young eels and gain colour.

On their way back to the rivers the young eels will meet and overcome all kinds of obstacles, climb up waterfalls and even wriggle across a damp field to reach a new stretch of water. At their freshwater homes they repeat the cycle of events carried out by their parents by staying for about ten years before setting off themselves to seek the spawning grounds and an end to life.

There are many other eels which belong to the same group as the freshwater eels, among them the conger, which lives and spawns in deep sea waters, and the fierce and ugly moray.

Salmon show extraordinary strength in overcoming obstacles such as river falls, up which they leap during their migrations.

The Salmon Family

Salmon are cold-water fishes, living in northern waters or rivers. Fully grown, they may be up to one and a half metres (four to five feet) long with an average top weight of 18 kilograms (40 pounds). But even larger specimens have been taken: a fish of 31 kilograms (70 pounds) has been recorded from the River Tay in Scotland. The most important game fish, salmon and trout, give wonderful sport to the angler: not only this, they are excellent to eat.

Although most fishes do not travel far from their original homes, some spend their lives almost constantly on the move, even though this movement is confined to a small area. Other species migrate from one place to another over long distances. The eel migrates from river to sea to spawn; the salmon does the same thing, only in reverse, leaving its home in the sea to spawn in rivers.

The pike waits for its victim.

This migratory urge is very strong and the salmon travels up to 3,200 kilometres (2,000 miles) to and from the Atlantic seas and the river of its birth. It begins life in shallow, fast-moving rivers and here it remains for a number of years. At this stage of its life it is called a parr. Just before it leaves the river to set off for the open sea it acquires a deposit on its skin which gives it a silvery sheen, and now the fish is known as a smolt.

It arrives in the Atlantic as an adult and lives there for from one to three years. Eventually, driven by the urge to spawn it sets off to find the river where it was born. In many cases, fishes do actually track down the exact stretch of water from which they came. Just how they do this is not known, although it is believed that a sense of smell guides them.

Records of the journeys of salmon are now being built up by means of tagging selected fish, rather in the way that bird movements are traced by means of ringed birds. The homing instinct of salmon is so strong that they will overcome all kinds of obstacles and they are capable of swimming against strong currents and of leaping up river falls.

Trout

There are various kinds of trout, some of which are migratory and others which spend their lives in freshwater lakes and rivers. The rainbow trout is a native of North America which has been introduced into European rivers. The grayling and the smelt are unusual in that their flesh gives off a pleasant scent. In the case of the grayling this has inspired its scientific name, *Thymallus*, a reference to the plant thyme, which its smell is said to resemble.

The Japanese Ayu, or sweetfish, a relative of the salmon family, is the object of a unique form of fishing. The Japanese train cormorants to go with them in their boats to catch the fish in their beaks. A bird is prevented from swallowing the fish by means of a metal ring placed around its neck.

Seen below are: 1 chub, 2 gudgeon, 3 char, 4 rudd, 5 minnow, 6 roach, 7 dace, 8 barbel, 9 carp, 10 grayling. All are members of the carp family except the char and the grayling.

Pike

The pike has a slender body and is flat-snouted with strong teeth which curve inwards to prevent any creature escaping from its grip. Some have been caught measuring over one metre (four feet) and weighing 35 kilograms (77 pounds). The pike has been called a freshwater shark, for it is a greedy predator on all kinds of animal life. It lies motionless at the bottom of weed-choked lakes and rivers, blending with its background so that it becomes almost invisible.

Apart from eating other fish it will take worms, frogs, waterbirds, voles —almost any animal unlucky enough to stray near its lair. It is known throughout northern parts of Europe, Asia and America. Most of the stories about the great age of certain individual fish are legendary, the longest life-span ever recorded being about fifteen years.

Carp and Catfishes

The most familiar freshwater fishes throughout the world are members of the carp family. In addition to the carp itself it includes the roach, rudd,

Deep-sea fishes seen above are: *Diretmus argenteus*, 2 eel larva, 3 *Sternoptyx diaphana*, 4 roosterfish, 5 lantern fish, 6 snipe eel, 7 *Opisthoproctus soleatus*, 8 angler fish, 9 prawn, 10 rat-tail, 11 tripod.

tench, gudgeon, minnow, bream, dace, chub and loach. All of them are fishes which are popular with the fisherman as they provide good sport, fighting for their lives and testing the skill of the angler. In general, they have toothless jaws, with rows of grinding teeth at the back of their mouths. Many are flesh-eaters but some feed on vegetation.

Goldfish belong to the carp family and their popularity as pets in home aquaria and garden ponds has led to the controlled breeding of a variety of forms, some weird, some beautiful. They came to the western world from China and Japan.

The family of catfishes is large and they are distinguished by pairs of barbels around their mouths which look rather like thick whiskers and so prompt their name. It is possible that like a cat's whiskers the barbels are used by the fish to help it move about and find food. The majority of catfishes live in the river estuaries of tropical countries.

Deep-sea Fishes

There is a mystery about the depths of the oceans and the creatures that live there which no amount of scientific enquiry will ever entirely dispel. Even the animals we know, which live in dark water beyond the reach of the sun's light, are frightening enough in appearance. But what weird things may still lurk unknown and unseen in the abyss of the oceans? There have always been tales of giant squids and fabled sea-monsters like the kraken, which rise up out of the water to crush boats and destroy human life, and it is difficult to feel confident that such tales have no basis in fact. However, most known animals which live in the depths of the sea are quite small.

In the lower parts of the sea not only is there little or no light, but enormous pressures build up which animals can only counteract by equal pressures within their bodies. If one of these deep-sea dwellers came rapidly to the surface it would burst as the balance of pressures changed.

The microscopic deep-sea plankton lives on dead animals and plant material which drops to the sea bed. In its turn this plankton becomes the food of many deep-sea creatures. Others feed directly from the organic material of larger creatures which die and sink to the bottom.

Fishes have developed a variety of special features to fit them for life in deep water. One is the enlargement of the eyes to obtain maximum vision in almost total blackness. Another is the expanding stomach which many species have, allowing them to swallow prey much bigger than themselves and to digest it over a long period, so that one meal may last a long time. A natural development of this function is the huge gaping mouth which many species have to help them swallow these gigantic meals.

The Angler Fish

The deep-water angler fish, which has been caught over 3,048 metres (10,000 feet) down, is one of the strangest members of a curious company. It has enormous jaws with backward pointing teeth and a luminous bait on its nose. The female angler fish is a giant compared with

Flying fish are capable of skimming across the surface of water. This is due to the impetus of a leap from the water rather than actual flight.

the male. When the tiny male meets up with a female (not an easy job since it depends on a chance encounter in total darkness in a vast featureless underwater landscape) he attaches himself to the underside of her body with his mouth and literally becomes a part of his partner. He loses not only his identity but his ability to function independently.

The Cod Family

The order of fishes to which the cod belongs contains a number of species which are caught and eaten by man. Fortunately, they are an abundant group, well able to survive the attentions of large-scale commercial fishing. The most familiar fish, apart from the cod, are hakes, haddocks and whiting. They all prefer the cold Arctic waters and are at their most numerous in the North Atlantic near the Dogger Bank and off the coasts of Iceland and Newfoundland.

The cod itself is generally between 60 and 120 centimetres (two and four feet) in length and about five kilograms (twelve pounds) in weight, although some fish of monster size have been caught which tipped the scales at ninety kilograms (200 pounds). The hake is a particularly greedy fish with a great liking for pilchard. When caught in a pilchard net it has been known to eat itself to a standstill even as the fishermen were gathering the catch. The haddock can be distinguished readily from its cousins by the blackish patch on each side of the body above the pectoral fin.

As well as the familiar fishes in this group there are related types which are comparatively unknown although some, like the rat-tails, are among the most numerous of deep-water fishes.

The Stickleback

Sticklebacks take their name from the isolated spines on their backs, which vary in number, generally from three to nine. They are mainly freshwater fish although there is a sea-stickleback. This marine species has as many as fifteen spines and has the distinction of being one of the few 'annual' vertebrates, since it usually dies within a year of its birth. Sticklebacks are very aggressive fish and the males engage in constant fights with each other, particularly at breeding time when favoured areas are being disputed. Two fish will dart at each other, attacking, retreating and feinting like a pair of wrestlers, until they grip one another in a stranglehold from which one fish will emerge the victor.

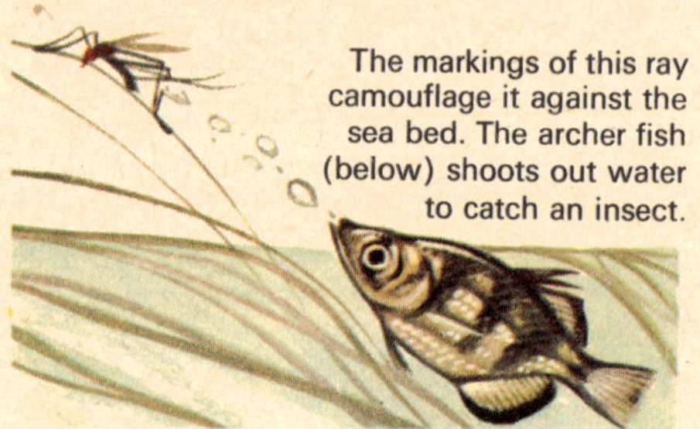
The markings of this ray camouflage it against the sea bed. The archer fish (below) shoots out water to catch an insect.

They have the interesting habit of nest-building, unusual in fishes. Some of these nests are made from weeds carefully bound together with a silk-like thread. In a single nest, eggs are laid by several females. The male stickleback also develops a breeding coloration in which parts of its body assume a reddish tinge.

The Perch Tribe

The vast order of perches and their allies includes most of the marine fishes. They breed in great quantities and number in their midst two which are very important to the fishing industry, the mackerel and the tunny.

The common perch is a handsome creature, its scales shading from greenish-brown to golden and white. It is a flesh-eater and exists largely on minnow, dace and other young fish, as well as worms and insects.

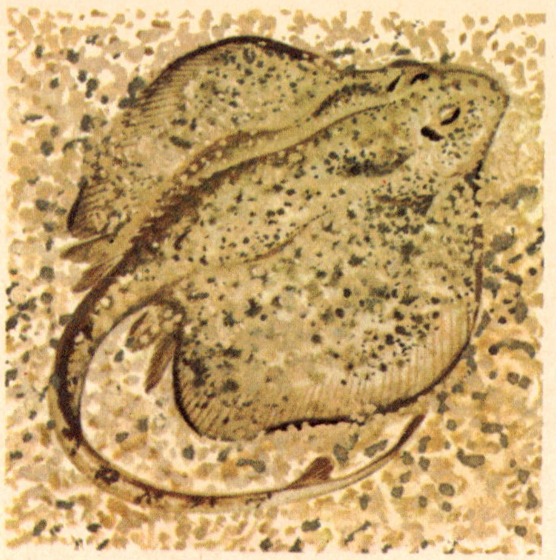

There are many other familiar species in the group, including bass, mullet and bream.

One of the oddities is the climbing perch which lives in Indian waters. Its pectoral fins are used as limbs and with them it drags itself across land for considerable distances. Whether it actually climbs trees is doubtful but certainly in wet weather it has been seen to clamber over

The coelacanth is a type of primitive fish which lived about 300 million years ago. Scientists believe it has not changed for the past 200 million years. Although it was thought to have been extinct for a very long time, a specimen was dragged up by a trawler fishing off the coast of East Africa in 1938. Other specimens of this living fossil have since been caught in tropical waters around India and Africa.

rain-soaked branches and other obstacles. It has a special organ which allows it to breathe for periods on land. Also related to the perch is the mudskipper, another fish which is well adapted to an existence out of water. It has very prominent, close-set eyes which can be protruded and retracted and a well-developed outer eyelid. As it lumbers across the ground, snapping at flies and raising itself on its pectoral fins as if they were elbows to peer around, it looks like an oversized newt.

Mackerel have specially beautiful colouring with bluish-green scales and a belly of iridescent silver. They congregate in shoals of immense size and have seasonal migrations when they leave the open sea and swim towards the shore to look for food. Mackerel are pelagic fishes (from the Greek word *pelagos* for the sea), that is, they live near the surface of the water and are caught in drift nets. The other great class of marine fish,

Colour in fishes is used for camouflage and display. Brightly coloured sea creatures such as these butterfly fishes usually live in tropical waters, often around a coral reef.

to which cod belong, are called demersal (from the Latin word *demergere*, to sink) and they live on or near the sea bed and are usually caught by trawling.

Relatives of the mackerel are the tunny or tuna fish and the bonito, both valuable to man as a source of food. The body temperature of the tunny is higher than that of the water in which it lives, a feature unique in fishes. Its blood system is highly developed to act as a temperature regulator.

Flatfishes

A remarkable example of adaptation to a chosen environment is seen in the flatfish, the well-known plaice, soles, dabs and flounders. The typical flatfish is compressed sideways because of its habit of living on the bottom of the sea. When a young fish is hatched it is more or less the normal shape with an eye on each side of its head. As it grows it develops the flat look of the adult fish. The front part of the skull is gradually twisted and one eye begins to move across the top of the head to lie alongside the other so that both are on one side of the body. It is thought that this adaptation was a gradual process in which the fish assumed a shape that suited its way of life. When flatfish are lying on the sandy bottom of the sea they merge almost completely with their background, the spots on their bodies helping to camouflage them, and so hide them from their enemies.

Amphibians

The name amphibian comes from some Greek words which mean 'living in two places'. This is an apt description of the animals called the amphibians, as they divide their lives between water and land. Today they are all small animals, the largest being the giant salamander of the Far East, which grows to a length of about one and a half metres (five feet), but in the prehistoric past they included some which grew to three and a half metres (twelve feet) long.

Today there are about 2,000 different species of amphibians, mostly living in the warmer and damper regions of the world. They can be classified into three groups: first the caecilians or blindworms, a small tropical group of burrowing animals; second the newts and salamanders; and third, the frogs and toads.

The typical amphibian starts life in the water. The pattern of mating behaviour varies greatly between the different species, but the eggs which are produced are usually laid in large numbers. In frogs and toads they are fertilised externally, after they have left the female's body. In newts, although there is internal fertilisation, often there is no direct contact between the pair. Many of the tropical amphibians have developed methods of protecting the eggs. They do this by making a nest in which the eggs hatch, or by providing parental protection, or by laying shelled eggs, or by producing living young. But in general the spawn has only a gelatinous outer covering. This is protective to some extent, but it soon becomes dried up if there is no water. And it is no help against the many predators, including fish and birds, which can make short work of amphibians' eggs.

The toad sits motionless when it is about to feed. When an insect is within reach it darts out its tongue and in a flash its prey is caught.

Tadpoles and Adults

Each egg has only a small yolk, so that the embryo has little resources for development and is forced to hatch within a few days. The creature which emerges from the egg is very different from its parents. Not only is it tiny, but in shape it resembles a fish, with external gills and a long tail which is used for swimming. The tadpole, as the larval stage is called, has to change greatly as it grows. The external gills are soon lost and within a few weeks tiny hind limbs appear, followed by forelimbs. As it grows the tail diminishes in the frog group, until finally the little creature has changed completely to its adult form. An important internal change has also taken place in the digestive system, for tadpoles are plant-eaters, while adult amphibians are flesh-eaters and have a completely different type of gut.

The dangers of life are not over with metamorphosis, as the change from tadpole to adult is called, for many creatures–including mammals, birds, snakes and fishes–are always willing to make a meal of frogs or newts. Very few of the young amphibians survive to breed themselves. A peril greater than their natural enemies has recently beset them and this is the danger of chemical pollution. Amphibians have very small lungs and part of their breathing is through their soft, moist skin. This cannot prevent the entry into their bodies of many chemicals used today in agriculture, which are usually lethal to the animals. Amphibians of all kinds have decreased drastically in numbers wherever modern agricultural practices occur.

European fire salamander

Lines of Defence

Helpless as they appear to be in the face of enemies, the amphibians have a number of lines of defence. The most important are the poison glands in the skin, the largest of which lie just behind the head and can be seen quite easily in toads and some salamanders. When stimulated they produce a whitish fluid, which is extremely irritating to the eyes, mouth and nose of any animal investigating the amphibian too closely. In some species in which these glands are well developed a pattern of warning colouration also occurs. The fire salamander of mainland Europe, for example, has dazzling yellow and black colours, a clear warning to predators not to attack. Any animal which is foolish enough to do so will have a very unpleasant experience, and will remember the general colour pattern and avoid similar looking animals in future.

Another defence, used by toads and frogs, is for the threatened animals to blow themselves up with air, often doubling their size in the process. This not only makes them look more fearful to the predator, but because the tissues are quite hard, like the surface of a fully inflated balloon, it may be much more difficult for a snake, say, to get a grip on a frog, which may eventually escape as a result.

All amphibians feed on insects, snails, worms, grubs, or even young of their own kind. They are capable of surviving long periods without food, but may be extremely greedy when it becomes available. Frogs and toads are able to shoot the tongue out a surprisingly long distance to catch an insect or other small animal which may be several inches away. This is possible because the tongue is hinged in the front of the mouth with the tip folded back towards the throat so it can be flicked out at a moment's notice to catch the prey.

The ways in which animals develop often show similarities which are proof of close relationship, even when the adults are very unalike. The reverse is true and the different development patterns of frogs and newts show the marked difference between the two groups. The rate of growth in both cases is affected by temperature, but under ideal conditions a common frog should have completed its change, or metamorphosis, in about four months. Some newts take longer. In the diagram below the stages of development of the frog (above) and the newt (below) are seen.

Secretive Animals

Although amphibians are widespread they frequently go unnoticed as they are small, secretive animals, keeping on the whole to moist places. In the temperate areas of the world they are forced to hibernate in the winter time, which takes them further from man's eyes. The only occasion when they make themselves obvious is during the breeding season, when large numbers of them travel to their traditional breeding ponds, sometimes congregating from an area of several square kilometres. Exactly what draws them is unknown, but it is thought that the algae in the water, which is the essential food for the tadpoles, may have a faint but very distinctive smell which attracts the animals. It is at this time of year that the frogs and toads become especially vocal, singing their trilling or croaking songs almost incessantly.

The newts may change colour, the males developing a bright orange display dress and large crests which run along the back and tail. In the crested newt this is particularly noticeable, for it forms a jagged ridge, broken at the base of the tail, which increases the size of the animal considerably. In the palmate newt, the crest is smoother but continuous. In both species it is lost after the breeding season, and at other times of the year all that is visible is a low ridge running the length of the animal's back. The purpose of these changes of colour and shape is to attract the females, for the newts perform complicated dances before breeding.

Spotted salamander

Salamanders and newts retain their tails throughout life, unlike frogs and toads, and are lizard-like in appearance.

Long-tailed salamander

Yellow-blotched salamander

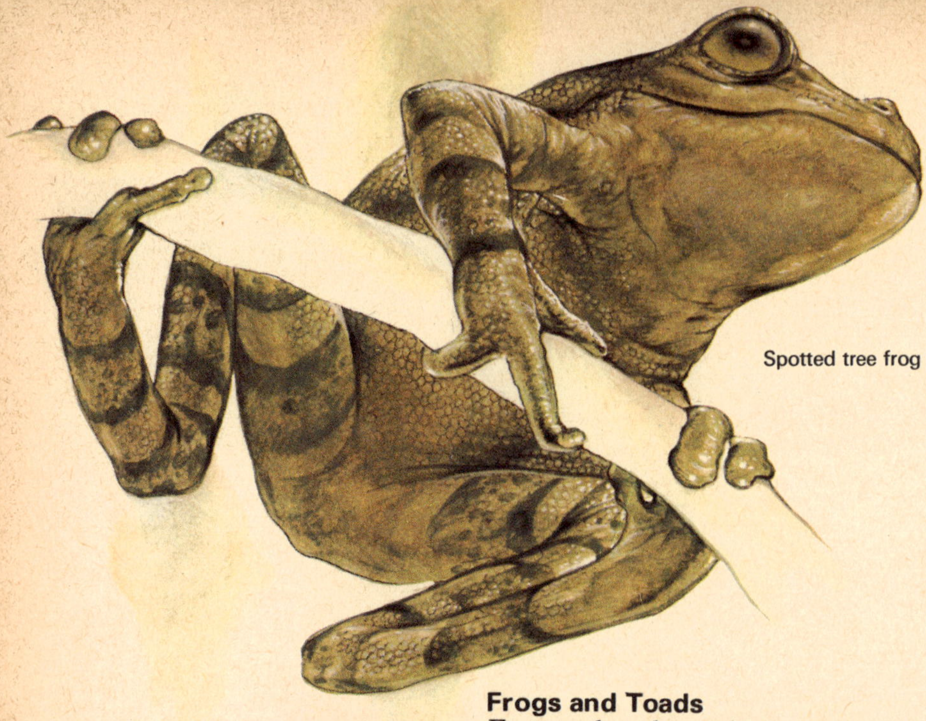

In size they range from the giant goliath frog, which is about 300 millimetres (one foot) long, and can tackle prey as large as a rat, to tiny tree frogs only about 25 millimetres (one inch) long. Many of them are long-lived and there are records of pet toads having survived forty years in a garden. The poison glands of the skin are well developed in most toads, but the dendrobates frog is one of the most venomous of the group. An extract of the skins of these little animals is so poisonous that it was once used by certain South American Indians to tip their arrows for hunting or wars.

Spotted tree frog

Dendrobates frog

Frogs and Toads

Frogs and toads are the most successful of the present day amphibians and are to be found in many environments throughout the world. They are quite unlike the newts in appearance, for they are all tail-less and all have hind legs very much longer than their forelimbs. Their usual method of movement is by hopping, although a few species can run. The distinctions between frogs and toads are internal and the terms are often used very loosely, but in general frogs have slenderer bodies and smoother skins, while toads have a more thickset appearance and drier, warty skins.

Climbing Frogs

Many frogs of the warmer parts have developed the ability to climb, and spend much time in the trees. Peron's tree frog, an Australian species, is in many ways typical. It is never found very far from water and has webbed fingers and toes, which help it as a swimmer. It has also developed large adhesive discs on each finger and these enable it to climb, so it may be found in trees and bushes from where its loud mating calls are often heard. Some climbing frogs have large webbed feet which are spread and used as parachutes when the animal jumps from one tree to another.

Common toad

Borneo flying frog

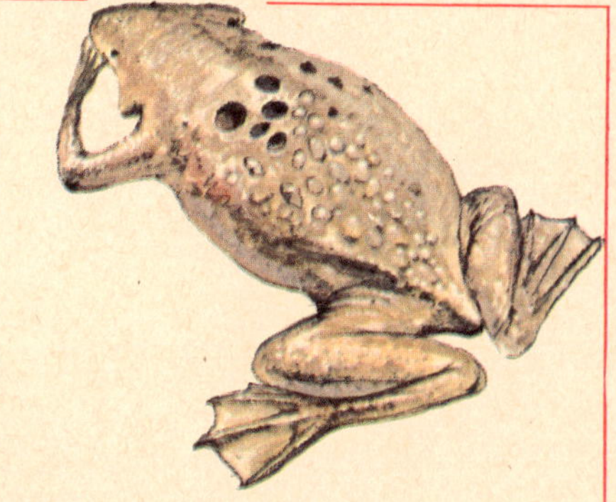

The Surinam Water Toad

Many kinds of frogs have developed ways of protecting their helpless young during the larval stage. The Surinam water toad has a complete system. The eggs, after laying and fertilisation, pass upwards towards the back of the female. The skin has become specially thickened during the breeding season and the eggs stick to this for a little while, before sinking into pits which form as a result of the chemical reaction between the egg and the skin. Before long the eggs are entirely hidden from the outside world as a lid forms over the top of the pit. In this position the young develop safely on their mother's back eventually hatching as complete toads.

South American giant toad

Reptiles

Present day reptiles are the remnants of a group which was once dominant, containing some of the most bizarre and the biggest animals which have ever walked the earth. These cold-blooded scaly animals are now disliked by most people yet they are sometimes beautiful and often useful to man. But they are persecuted because of lack of knowledge of their nature and ways of life.

Reptiles are animals of the warm parts of the world. They are cold-blooded, which is to say that they have no control of their body temperature, and their energy is dependent on the temperature of their surroundings. If this is high the reptiles warm up and their bodily chemistry can proceed at a rate which ensures a rapid turnover of energy; if it is low the reptile becomes torpid and may be unable to move. Within this restriction, however, the reptiles occupy the world very fully. They are to be found in wet and dry tropical regions, as burrowers, tree-dwellers and water-dwellers. There are even some which lead a marine life and never come ashore, although they are air-breathing, like all other reptiles.

Egg Laying

The majority of reptiles lay eggs. These are fertilised internally, and are then laid on land, sometimes in a specially prepared nest but more usually in a protected place; under a fallen log or among leaves, for example. The eggs, which are very much like birds' eggs in construction, have an outer shell, which may be hard or parchment-like. Inside the egg the embryo develops using the food supply of the large yolk, buffered and protected by the albumen, or white, which is also used as it grows. Compared with birds' eggs, in which development of the chick is rapid, growth within the reptile egg is very slow. The egg of a Greek tortoise may take three months to hatch; a comparably sized bird's egg takes about three weeks. During this time, however, the embryo passes through its tadpole stages, and it hatches as a miniature, recognisable replica of its parents.

Although in a few cases the mother may remain near the eggs, once they have hatched her responsibilities cease and she takes no interest in the young, which are fully equipped to look after themselves. Some reptiles, especially those living in a somewhat unfavourable environment, retain the eggs inside the body of the female until they are ready to hatch. The young are then born alive, or within a very flimsy shell from which they escape immediately.

Eating and Movement

With their low turnover of energy, reptiles do not need to feed often. Many are flesh-eaters, but quite a large proportion eat plant food. Reptile teeth are all the same shape round the mouth, so biting and thorough chewing of the food does not occur as it does in mammals, and each mouthful is swallowed with very little mastication. Digestion is slow and many reptiles are capable of going several months between meals.

Reptiles often give the impression of moving very fast and indeed a lizard scuttling for shelter if danger threatens may be travelling quite quickly. On the whole, however, they are incapable of sustained activity, and when they run they throw their bodies into curves which may give a greater illusion of speed than is justified. This sinuous movement is because reptiles always use alternate limbs and cannot, however fast they wish to go, gallop, as mammals do. In legless reptiles such as snakes and slow-worms the sinuous movement is exaggerated and they appear to loop across the ground.

In the past many kinds of reptiles which were fairly fast moving became bipedal; that is they used their hind legs only, for their forelimbs were too small for weight bearing. A reptile which adopts this pose is the Australian frilled lizard. When frightened this animal rises on to its hind legs, and balancing its body with its tail, which curves up until it almost touches the head, it can run at a considerable speed for some distance. If it is finally cornered its last line of defence is to turn and stand, with its mouth defiantly open, and to spread a large fan of skin around its head. This makes it look bigger and fiercer than it really is and may deter a predator from pressing home an attack.

Methods of attack and defence used by reptiles vary—some snakes and a very few lizards are poisonous, but hardly any are aggressive and some which are venomous have warning colouration to give clear notice of the fact.

The frilled lizard frightens its enemies by expanding a frill round its neck.

Giant Galapagos tortoise

Common tortoise

Indian starred tortoise

Tortoises and Turtles

Although there are more than 200 different kinds of tortoises found throughout the warmer parts of the world, they are among the easiest of animals to recognise, for they all wear the most complete armour plating protection to be found anywhere among the land vertebrates. The naming of these animals is confused, however. In Britain, where there are no native members of the group, the term tortoises is generally used for land-dwellers, terrapins for freshwater-dwellers, and turtles for the marine species. In America, where many species occur, the word turtle is used very much more widely and terrapin has a much more restricted meaning.

The shell which all of these animals carry forms a box, made in two parts, an upper and a lower. Both are made of bony plates, overlaid by horny shields. The edges of the bone and horn plates overlap, so that the whole armour has a great deal of strength.

Growth Rings

Those species which live in the colder areas, such as the European pond tortoise, which is found in southern Europe, hibernate in the winter time and, because of this, they grow irregularly. This is reflected in the pattern of their horny plates, which show growth rings like trees, so that their age may be gauged by counting the rings. This is not an entirely reliable method of telling the age of a tortoise, for illness or injury which cause checks in growth look like age rings. When the animal ages, its growth slows up and it may not be easy to read the rings, which are very narrow, and wear may also make it more difficult. There is no doubt, though, that tortoises can live to a great age; one which was taken from the Seychelles to Mauritius in 1766 did not die until it was accidentally killed in 1918, at an age well over 150 years. Smaller species live for a much shorter time, but for longer than mammals of a comparable size.

The two halves of the shell are joined along the sides, but in many species the legs, head and tail can be pulled in under the protective covering.

Marine turtles come ashore each year to lay their eggs then return to the sea.

Box turtles have a hinge in the shell which folds up so that in time of danger the animal is completely shut in—a mechanism which defeats most predators. Land tortoises, such as the star tortoise, usually have a heavy high-domed shell; water tortoises usually have a lighter, flatter shell and often cannot withdraw their limbs into it. Land tortoises have a club-footed appearance; whereas in terrapins the toes are separate but connected with a web of skin. Marine turtles have limbs which form strong paddles for swimming.

The route of the *Beagle* around the Galapagos Islands.

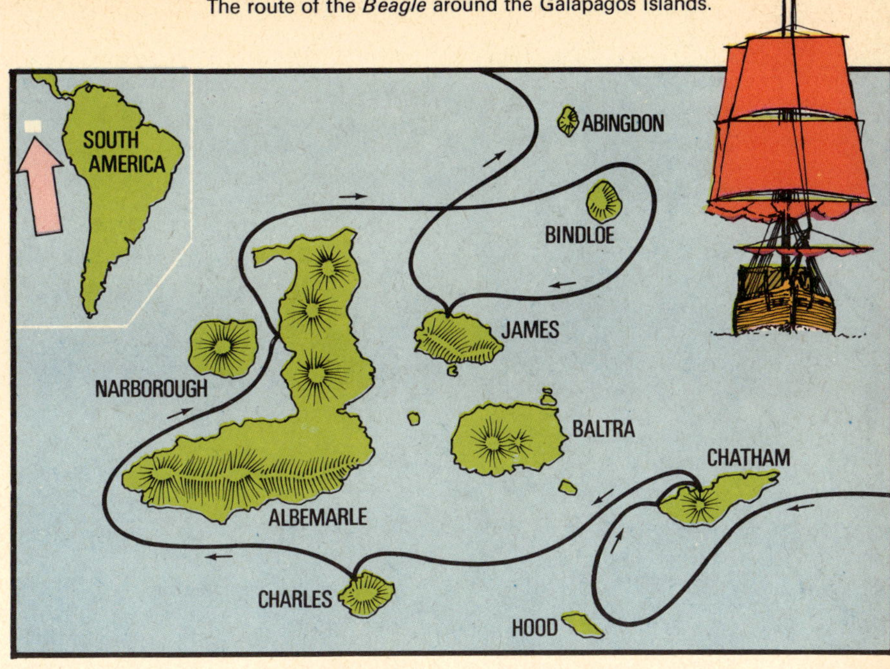

In 1835 the British ship the *Beagle* called at the Galapagos Islands in the Pacific, during a round-the-world survey. On board was a young naturalist called Charles Darwin. On the isolated volcanic Galapagos Islands he observed that there were many species of animal which, although obviously related to other forms on the mainland, were different in some vital respects. He saw that this was especially so with the giant tortoises which were recognisably different on separate islands. This set him thinking that the isolation had a bearing on their differences. This idea was elaborated into the theory of evolution through natural selection. The Galapagos tortoises are now almost extinct.

Slow Movement

Although the shell is protective, it brings many drawbacks. Chief of these is the weight, which makes tortoises proverbial slowcoaches. Other difficulties are caused because the shell bones are fused with the ribs and the vertebrae; the body has become a rigid box; the strong muscles of the back are lost and movement is clumsy as well as slow. Tortoises cannot expand their chests when they breathe; instead air has to be forced into their lungs by a pumping action of the throat. Some freshwater species, although they are chiefly air-breathing, can also make use of oxygen dissolved in the water, which is absorbed through special membranes in their mouths and their vents.

Tortoises and turtles are entirely without teeth. Instead the jaws are covered with horny shields which are scissor-sharp and enable the animals to cut up their food. The land-livers are mainly vegetarian, but the terrapins and turtles which live in water are mostly flesh-eaters. Sometimes these search out the worms and shrimps on which they feed, but some of the larger forms, which eat fish and other active animals, are amazingly well camouflaged to resemble weed-covered logs, so they can snap up anything which approaches them unawares.

Most land and freshwater tortoises are small animals; the giants of the group are the marine turtles, the largest being about two and a half metres (eight feet) long and weighing close to 900 kilograms (2000 pounds). These are slow and clumsy on land, but swim effortlessly and elegantly when buoyed up by sea water. They still show their land heritage by the fact that the females must come ashore each year to lay their eggs. Having mated in the water they arrive at night on sandy beaches where they scoop out a nest above the tide line. In this they lay a hundred or more eggs, before filling the nest in and scattering sand about to disguise its position.

Marine turtles move in water with a grace that belies their clumsy appearance.

Return to the Sea

They then return to the sea, which they must reach before the break of day. Having no means of controlling their body-temperature, turtles die if exposed for long to the heat of the sun. Although the nest position itself is hidden, the turtle's tracks down the beach are not. The presence of a tail drag-mark indicates that eggs have been laid and egg hunters may come and find the nest, despite its disguise. Many eggs are taken by human and other predators, and this, combined with the hunting of the adults, has led to a great decline in turtle numbers.

The biggest land tortoises are always found on oceanic islands. Many animals which are swept by chance to these isolated places evolve into strange forms, unknown elsewhere, and this is the case with the tortoises. The tortoises of Aldabra, the Mascarene islands and Galapagos for example, have all grown to gigantic size in the absence of predators or competitors for food.

Lizards and Snakes

The Komodo dragon

Lizards and snakes are the most abundant of the reptiles. Within the warm parts of the world they have occupied almost every type of habitat and are found as tree dwellers, burrowers and desert animals, and living in swamps and rivers. Generally the distinction between them is clear, for most lizards have sprawling legs while snakes are totally limbless. However, there are many legless lizards, such as the slow-worm, and the external differences between these animals and some snakes may lie in details of their scale pattern.

The Ways of Lizards

Snakes and some lizards have forked tongues. Using them, the animals track their prey, tasting the trail as their tongues flicker out over the ground. The deep fork enables a wider area to be sampled than would be possible with a simpler shape. A lizard with a very extraordinary tongue is the chameleon. Living in trees, it feeds mainly on large insects, which it stalks cautiously to within several inches and then shoots out its long tongue to gather its prey on the end. The tongue is formed of elastic tissues, under compression when the mouth is closed.

The largest of all lizards is the Komodo dragon. This is related to the monitor lizards of the Old World, but living in isolation on its islands the Komodo has grown to a length of about three metres (ten feet). It is a powerful, slow moving, largely scavenging animal, far removed from the aerial monster of fables. The nearest that any lizard comes to flight is the gliding lizard, *Draco*, which has a web of skin along its sides. This is supported by extensions of the animal's ribs, which are hinged so that the membrane may be folded along the sides or held out stiffly as it leaps from one tree to another in a long, shallow glide.

Most lizards are small and often escape notice by their camouflage patterns or by their habit of hiding in crevices or under stones. Some are highly valued as destroyers of insects and the geckos, which are among the few noisy lizards, are welcome house animals in spite of this. These animals have feet on which a series of fine ridges of skin, like enlarged finger-prints, make each toe into a suction device so that they can run up walls and across ceilings in search of their prey.

The tails of lizards may serve many purposes. In some, such as the monitors, they are long and whip-like and may be used in defence. In other species which live in desert areas the tail is short and stumpy and carries reserves of food, which enables the animal to survive long periods of drought without eating or drinking. In the chameleons the tail is prehen-sile and acts as an extra hand for a

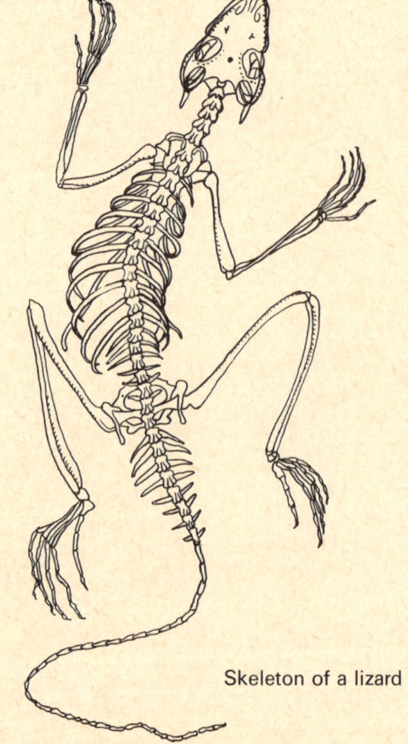
Skeleton of a lizard

The Tuatara
Reptiles, apart from snakes and lizards, may be regarded as living fossils, left over from a time when the earth was peopled with their kind. One reptile in particular is a relic from the past–the tuatara, a superficially lizard-like creature which is found only on islands off the coasts of New Zealand. Its skull bones show it to be related to a once widespread group, now extinct except for this one representative. It is a nocturnal, secretive animal, living in burrows. Recent researches have revealed that it is long-lived. The feature of a third eye on the top of its head, which may be light sensitive in young animals, is probably to do with a form of heat regulation, for they are more active at lower temperatures than most other reptiles.

The chameleon captures food with its long tongue.

Snakes wind their way across the ground in a series of graceful curves but never in up and down loops. On a smooth surface a snake is helpless and cannot make any progress. Over areas of loose sand some desert snakes 'sidewind', moving two loops of their bodies simultaneously but keeping the rest clear.

more secure grip on the branches over which the lizard climbs. In the majority of lizards, however, the tail is extremely fragile. Across one of the vertebrae is a plane of weakness and if any stress is put on this, the tail breaks at that point. Any predator which grabs the tail is likely to find that it has just that, while the lizard escapes to grow another tail from the broken end.

Snakes probably evolved their legless shape as burrowing animals. Now only pythons have any trace of limbs at all, and these are in no way functional. Yet snakes survive in a wide range of environments and can often climb or swim well. All snakes are flesh-eaters, but since their teeth are simply sharp hooks in the mouth, they cannot bite pieces of their food or chew it, so they are forced to swallow their prey whole. Their jaws can stretch so that they may gulp down creatures which may be bigger than themselves. The meal may take a long time and digestion even longer, for a small snack may last a snake for weeks or even months. Some snakes pursue their prey and catch and swallow it with no special adaptations. Others, such as the pythons and constrictors, throw a coil of their immensely strong bodies round the prey animal and suffocate it before they swallow it.

Poison Glands

A minority of snakes carry poison glands in their mouths. Although the poison is in many cases very powerful, few snakes are aggressive and most restrict its use to their prey alone, although if badly frightened they may use it in defence. Some snakes have very specialised food, some of the strangest being the egg-eating snakes. These slender inhabitants of the African bush swallow the eggs of ground-nesting birds and cut through the eggshell with a saw formed of the projecting tips of parts of the vertebrae in the throat. The shell is then ejected and the soft part of the egg swallowed. Between them, snakes feed on a wide variety of foods. Some feed on worms, some on other snakes, some on snails. Many are destroyers of rodent pests and as such should be valued.

The senses of snakes are limited and apart from their excellent senses of smell and taste they seem to be poorly endowed. Their eyesight is moderate, and they are totally deaf to air-borne sounds. Unlike lizards, which can hear well, snakes have no ears although they can detect vibrations coming from the ground through their jaw bones, so they can make their escape if a large and heavy animal approaches.

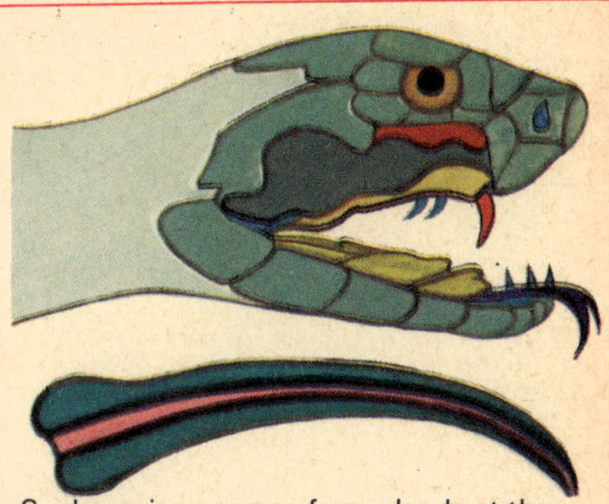

Snake poison comes from glands at the back of the upper jaw. It is then channelled down into the mouth. In some species, which are not normally considered very dangerous to man, the poison dribbles down teeth at the back of the palate. These back-fanged snakes have to take their prey right into their mouths before their poison can be effective. In snakes which have a more effective system, the venom is carried to the front of the mouth where it runs down enlarged fangs which ensure that the prey receives a dose of poison as it is bitten. In adders and rattlesnakes the poison fangs are hollow, like a hypodermic needle, so that the venom is injected with the bite. In these snakes the hollow teeth are so large that they have to be folded back when the jaw is closed.

As they grow, snakes and lizards shed their skins. In lizards this is done piecemeal; in snakes the skin is peeled off complete, and the snake, which for a few days has been looking dull and behaving rather listlessly, becomes more active in its new, brightly coloured scales. The cast skin may sometimes be found, complete even to the eye covering, looking like the scaly ghost of its one-time owner.

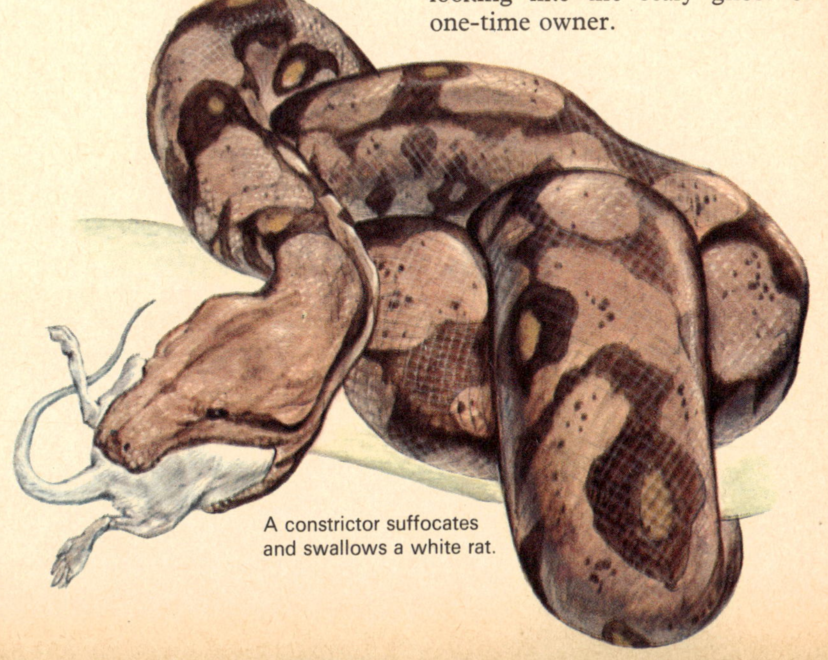

A constrictor suffocates and swallows a white rat.

Crocodiles

The largest of present day reptiles are to be found among the crocodiles. This seems fitting, for the twenty-five species are the sole survivors of a much larger group which in the distant past contained the dinosaurs. These were the largest reptiles ever to have lived and although no crocodile of today achieves their size, or ever has, there are records of animals up to seven metres (23 feet) long. Crocodiles are relentlessly hunted wherever they live and few really old animals which may approach maximum size now survive.

The favourite haunts of the Nile crocodile are sandbanks alongside rivers where the currents are sluggish. They are ferocious animals and some live to a great age.

Water Animals

Crocodiles and their close relatives are rarely found far from water. The estuarine crocodile, which lives on the coasts of south-east Asia and north Australia, is often seen well out to sea, although it is not as totally marine as were some fossil forms. Today crocodiles are normally seen sprawled on sandbanks in a river or estuary, or on the edge of a lake. Their normal movement is the typical ungainly gait of the land reptile, with the body swinging into curves as they progress. If pressed, however, a crocodile can pick itself up on to its toes and run, holding the body well clear of the ground. It can travel in a straight line in this way and moves quite surprisingly fast, but the animal cannot maintain this position or speed for long and tires quickly. Once in the water, the crocodile is transformed into a creature of speed and power. Becoming streamlined by folding its limbs back against the body, it uses its heavy flattened tail as an oar to scull along, scarcely rippling the water as it goes.

The crocodile's adaptation for its way of life may be seen in many features, but particularly in the head, in which the eyes and nostrils stand above the level of the rest of the face. This enables the animal to float, just submerged, but to be able to see and to continue breathing, while it stalks its prey unnoticed by potential meals or potential enemies. In most reptiles the nostrils open directly into the front of the mouth. In a crocodile the air is channelled, as it is in mammals, to a position in the back of the throat, leaving the mouth to be used for food alone. This enables it to catch and subdue prey under water, but to continue breathing, although the nostrils may be tightly closed if necessary.

Some large, old crocodiles may be a menace to man or his domestic stock, but their food for the greater part of their lives consists of insects, fish and rodents. In places where crocodiles have been exterminated, their prey animals have often increased to pest proportions. Crocodiles' teeth are sharp pegs unsuited to slicing or chewing food, which must, therefore, be swallowed whole. A big, old crocodile may tear limbs off a large victim by a twisting movement of its head. They certainly feed on the carrion bodies of drowned animals and having caught and killed

The crocodile is able to float near the surface of water with only its eyes and nostrils showing. Here it waits for prey.

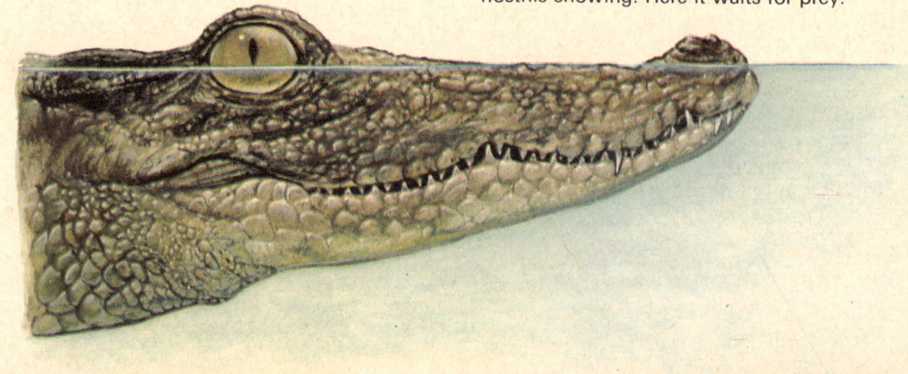

a bullock or some such creature, may sometimes hide it in a place where it will rot to some extent so that it may more easily be torn apart.

Breeding Habits

The breeding season is the only time when crocodiles become at all noisy. The brawling males may be heard over long distances and both males and females develop musky scent glands, the secretion from which probably repels rivals and attracts mates. All crocodiles reproduce by eggs. These may be deposited in a hollow scooped in the sand of a river bank or laid in a nest of rotting vegetation, which releases heat to help them hatch. In some cases they are protected by their mother who remains in the area of the nest, driving away egg-stealing intruders such as rodents and small carnivores. She may even, as in the Mississippi alligator, hear cries of the hatching young and help them by opening up the nest pile and then escorting them to the water.

From then on the young creatures are on their own and the greatest enemies many of them have to fear are the larger members of their own kind. Snapping and active from the start, they grow rapidly in their early years in spite of the lack of parental care. Even when they have achieved adult size they continue to grow, although increasingly slowly. A big crocodile may be many years old although it is unlikely that in the wild it will reach the very great age claimed for captive specimens.

The differences between crocodiles and alligators are slight and the terms are often used wrongly. The easiest way to tell them apart is to look at the teeth. The fourth tooth from the mid-line in the lower jaw is much larger than the rest. In crocodiles this is easily visible when the mouth is shut, for there is a notch in the upper jaw to house it. In alligators the tooth fits into a pit in the upper jaw and so is invisible when the mouth is closed.

In some parts of the world crocodiles are protected and even farmed, mainly for the high quality leather produced from their skins, but generally they are feared and hated. Wherever possible they are destroyed and it seems likely that in many areas the crocodiles will follow the dinosaurs into extinction. In spite of this they are sometimes kept as aquarium animals, occasionally growing to an embarrassing size under such protected conditions.

Gavials and false gavials, although not closely related, appear similar because of their long slender snouts. These are fish traps, provided with a battery of narrow, interlocking teeth. These animals sweep their heads from side to side through schools of fish, which are their only food.

The Mississippi alligator's nearest relative is the Chinese alligator. It is very unusual for two closely related animals to be found on opposite sides of the world with no connecting links, and no satisfactory explanation has been offered. Caimans are distantly related to crocodiles.

Birds

Birds, the last of the vertebrate classes to evolve, have certainly made up for lost time, for there are now nearly 9,000 bird species, compared to about only 3,200 kinds of mammals. Like the mammals, birds are active, warm-blooded animals, but their great specialisation is flight, which has enabled them to colonise many places unavailable to earthbound creatures.

Many of the modifications which have been made to achieve flight can be seen in the skeleton, which has the same basic elements as that of other land vertebrates. It is extremely lightly built, for like any other flying machine a bird cannot afford to carry unnecessary weight, so the limb bones are hollow, although they may be braced with internal struts for strength. The main part of the body is supported by a bony box, very strongly constructed, which carries the muscles for flight attached to the deep ridged breastbone. This box must also be strong to absorb the jar as a bird lands and to carry the hind limbs, which in most species are relatively small. They are however given extra length by the fact that birds stand on their toes—what we think of as a bird's knee is really its ankle.

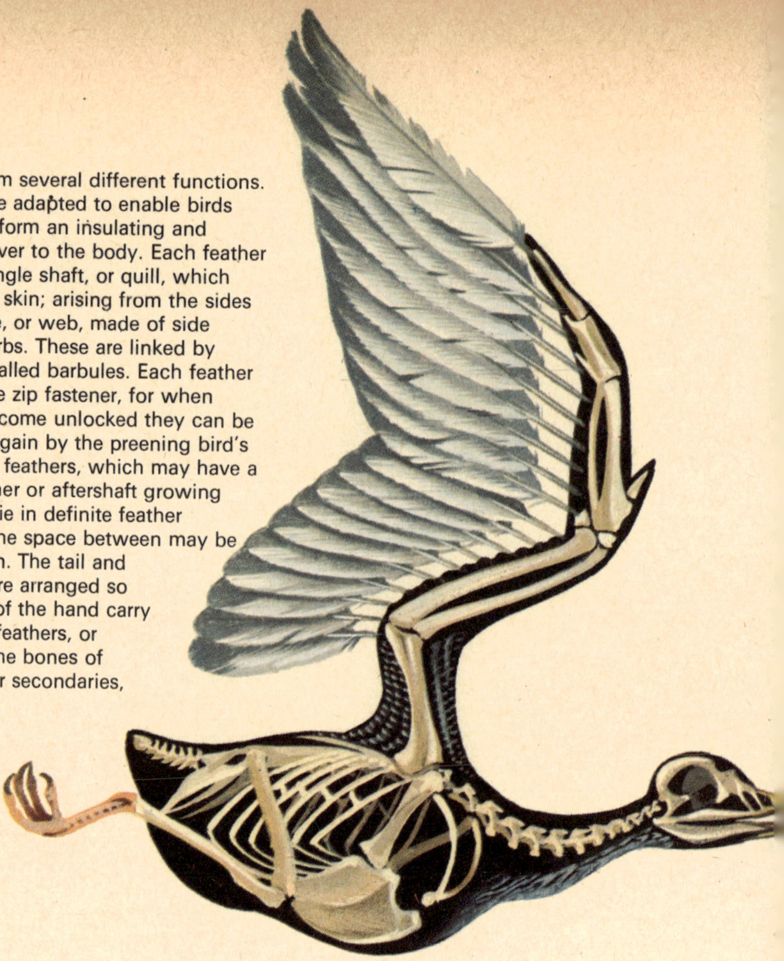

Feathers perform several different functions. Chiefly, they are adapted to enable birds to fly and they form an insulating and streamlining cover to the body. Each feather consists of a single shaft, or quill, which grows from the skin; arising from the sides of this is a vane, or web, made of side struts called barbs. These are linked by minute hooks called barbules. Each feather is like a multiple zip fastener, for when the barbules become unlocked they can be fixed together again by the preening bird's beak. The body feathers, which may have a subsidiary feather or aftershaft growing from the base, lie in definite feather tracts, though the space between may be filled with down. The tail and wing feathers are arranged so that the bones of the hand carry the main flight feathers, or primaries, and the bones of the forearm bear secondaries, or lift, feathers.

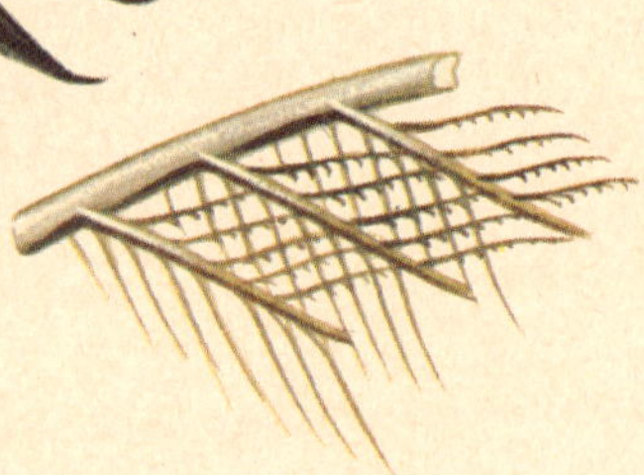

The Organs of Flight

The forelimbs are normally much bigger, for these are the organs of flight. The bones can be compared to those of a human arm. The top bone of the forelimb is usually short and stout, and the outer and inner bones are well developed. The bones of the hand and fingers are to a large extent fused to make a strong base for the flight feathers, or primaries, which are attached to them. There is a separate 'thumb' bone to which a small bunch of feathers called the alula is fixed. This is raised and helps to control air flow over the wings at slow speeds and prevent stalling on take-off.

The skull is fairly big and contains a brain which, while not giving the bird much intellectual power, does allow large centres for sight, hearing, balance and co-ordination. The eyes of birds are large and they have very sharp vision, with a well developed sense of colour in most cases. Birds' ears are on the sides of their heads although not visible externally, and they hear very well. At the front of the skull is the beak, which is sheathed in horny material and contains no teeth. The shape of the beak varies according to the food eaten. It may be like a fine forceps for picking up small insects, or a notched knife for tearing flesh or a heavy nutcracker for dealing with large seeds. Birds see or hear their food or prey, for, with one exception, they have no sense of smell and their sense of taste is very limited.

At the other end of the skeleton the tail bones are fused to form a ploughshare bone. However long a bird's tail may be the feathers all fan out from this.

Flying Machines

Birds obey many of the physical rules applying to flying machines in general. Flight is hard work, so they need large amounts of food to fuel themselves. Digestion is quick and very complete; it is not possible by looking at a bird's droppings to tell what food has been eaten, as may be done with many mammals. Flying machines and birds need a great deal of oxygen and birds' lungs work on a system which gives them a constant stream of air rather than being inflated and deflated as is the case with mammals. Insulated by their feathers, they need to prevent themselves from overheating. They do this by means of air sacs which receive the air as it is first breathed in and pass it on to the lungs after it has been used in the cooling system. The heartbeat of birds is rapid and their temperature high compared to that of most mammals. Their high turnover of energy makes them physically the most efficient of the vertebrates.

Flightless Birds

Among the many roles which birds play, few conflict directly with mammals. Some birds, however, have developed as grazing animals. These are to be found mainly in tropical grassland areas throughout the world alongside mammalian competitors. These birds are large and heavyweight creatures, incapable of flight, but able to run very fast. Their wings are tiny—those of an ostrich, which may be two and a half metres (eight feet) tall and weigh 136 kilograms (300 pounds), are smaller in area than those of a goose. They have no need for flight muscles and there is no deeply ridged breastbone as in most birds. Instead, they have a flat plate of bone and for this reason are called the raft-breasted birds or ratites. Although so different in many ways from flying birds, details of their structure prove that they have descended from ancestors which were capable of flight.

The largest of the ratites are now extinct. Some species of moa from New Zealand reached a height of four metres (thirteen feet), and finds of giant bird bones on the island of Madagascar gave rise to legends in Arab mythology of the roc, or elephant bird.

The Ratites

Most present day ratites are sombre coloured birds, the exception being the male ostrich which has white wing and tail plumes contrasting with his black body feathers. Most have some degree of social behaviour during the breeding season, when several females may lay their eggs in the same nest, and where the males take a large part in incubation. The large eggs of ratites are sought by many predators, some of which have developed ingenious methods for breaking the thick shell. The chicks are active as soon as they leave the egg and many of them fall to flesh-eaters of various kinds.

The ostrich is the most familiar of the ratites, for it is often seen in zoos. Hunted for its plumes, it has decreased greatly in numbers, although it is farmed in some areas of South Africa. In the wild it is often found with herds of antelope and zebra, where it acts as a watchman, for it has far sharper eyesight than the mammals. In South America there are several species of rhea—wary, fast-running birds, which use their rudimentary wings for balance when turning at speed. These also have become much rarer than they were, through hunting and because their home range has been taken for cattle and sheep.

Australasian Birds

The national bird of Australia is the emu, yet another grazing ratite and again one that has been drastically reduced because it competes with introduced domestic mammals. In some areas the emu is now protected, but elsewhere there is still a bounty on its head and it is ruthlessly destroyed. In the tropical forests of North Australia and New Guinea the cassowary can be found. This large bird is among the best armed of the flightless species, for its inner toenail is a huge spike of horn with which it can protect itself.

In New Zealand lives the smallest and strangest of the ratites. This is the kiwi, which is a nocturnal, secretive creature with a long down-curved bill with which it probes out the worms and other invertebrates on which it feeds. It is unique in that it smells out its prey and is the only bird to have this ability.

The ratites are by no means the only birds which cannot fly. A number of species have lost the power to do so, although in general they have kept the features which are characteristic of flying birds. All have feathers, and all have the remnants of wings. Flightless birds are often found on islands, which are windy places, so that birds with a

The rhea is sometimes called the American ostrich. The plumage colour of the male and female birds is somewhat similar. In their native land they merge readily with the general colouring of the South American pampas so as to be almost invisible, even when they are in the middle distance.

strong tendency to fly are often swept away, but those with a tendency to flightlessness survive. Examples of the end product of this trend are the now extinct dodo and solitaire birds and such isolated rarities as the Gough Island rail, a secretive non-flying bird of a southern Atlantic island.

Intermediate stages between flight and flightlessness may be seen in two of the inhabitants of different types of environment. The bustards of the plains, for example, typify heavy-weight birds which run rather than fly whenever possible, although they still have functional wings. Birds living near water may also tend towards flightlessness and many of them have small wings which are used as much for swimming as for flying.

Penguins

Penguins are the best known flightless water birds. Their wings have become stiff, flattened paddles, which can no longer be folded in the normal way when the bird is at rest. Instead they hang like arms beside the body, which with the upright stance of penguins increases their likeness to small human figures. Penguins are found throughout the oceans of the southern hemisphere; the most northerly species nests on the Galapagos Islands, which sit astride the equator, but the better known species come from the Antarctic.

The harshness of their environment has caused the two largest species, the emperor and the king penguins, to have modified their breeding behaviour in most drastic ways. There is no material for nest building, so the egg is held on the feet of the male and covered with a protective flap of skin. It takes a long time for the eggs to hatch and both these birds have developed different ways of meeting the demands which this makes on them at nesting time. King penguins return to their breeding rookeries at a later time each year, for the period taken in caring for the chick, followed by the time for moulting and building up their resources again, is more than one year. Finally a year comes when they cannot complete the cycle of rearing a chick and the parents set off for the sea early, but are among the first of the breeding birds to return in the next season. With this staggered breeding pattern they may manage on average to rear two young in every three years.

Emperor Penguins

Emperor penguins prolong their breeding season by starting to nest at the beginning of the coldest of the dark winter months. So harsh is the weather that the birds have given up territorial behaviour and huddle together for communal warmth. The female returns to take her share of chick care just as the egg hatches and the male goes off to the sea to break his two months' fast. As the chick grows and becomes more demanding, the shelf ice melts and the parents have only a short journey to make to collect food for it.

Adélie penguins nest near the sea in places where the wind sweeps the snow away early. In such barren areas there is no nest material for them, so they raise their eggs above the level of any water on a little pile of stones. In this apparently comfortless condition their fluffy chicks are raised through the Antarctic summer months.

Emperor penguin

Rock-hopper

Adélie penguin

The origin of the name penguin is not known for certain. Possibly it comes from the term 'pin-wing', short for pinioned, meaning 'cut-wing', a name given by sailors to a black and white flightless bird of the north Atlantic, the great auk. This bird was similar to the penguins in its appearance and way of life. When whalers and sealers first went to southern polar waters they thought the birds there were the same as the ones in the north. Like penguins, the great auks congregated in vast breeding rookeries and hundreds of thousands of them were killed in the eighteenth century. The species eventually became extinct in 1844.

From left to right, a red-throated grebe, a black-throated diver and a crested grebe.

Petrel

Water Birds

Among freshwater birds there are no exact parallels to the extreme adaptations of the penguins. Grebes and divers are the most highly specialised for a life in fresh water. Both have their legs placed very far back on the body. This makes swimming more efficient, but they cannot stand upright like penguins and are helpless on land. The only time that divers come ashore is during the breeding period and their nests are within inches of the water; grebes make floating nests and never normally leave the water. Divers have webbed feet; grebes have each toe separately lobed with a stiff fin. Both dive and swim expertly under water and both can, in times of danger, expel the air from their feathers and sink from sight slowly and with no disturbance.

The great crested grebe is a handsome bird which was much in demand by the plumage trade in the early years of this century. Its numbers have been increased by protection and it is now a fairly common inhabitant of many stretches of inland water. In winter time the red-necked grebe might be mistaken for it, but this bird rarely moves from eastern Europe. The black-throated diver, like all the members of its group, is a northern bird. In winter when it loses its breeding plumage and migrates south it can be distinguished from its near relatives by the slender straight shape of its bill.

The longest winged of all birds are the albatrosses. The thirteen species of these giant tube-nosed birds are found in the southern oceans, apart from three Pacific species which cross the equator during migration after their breeding season. Mostly, they ride the winds effortlessly in the zone of the roaring forties, feeding on the abundant fish and plankton of that area and migrating huge distances yearly. Their breeding places are remote islands which are the only dry land that they ever encounter. They are slow-maturing and long-lived. According to some estimates, albatrosses reach ages of as much as seventy years.

Tubenoses

An important group of seabirds is the tubenoses, so called because the bill is covered with horny plates and the nostrils lie in a tunnel which they form. Included among them are the petrels, shearwaters, fulmars and albatrosses. All have long narrow wings adapted to make use of the quirky air currents over the disturbed waters of the sea. Petrels are mostly small, dark-coloured birds, which look as though they are pattering over the surface of the waves.

Shearwaters and fulmars bank and glide. Albatrosses have a superb control of the air, scarcely moving their wings yet staying aloft and making progress under all sorts of conditions. None of these birds ever comes to land except during the breeding season. The shearwaters, which have their legs set very far back on their bodies and cannot stand upright, nest in burrows to which they return at night and where they are protected from enemies such as gulls.

The gannets, pelicans and cormorants belong to an order of birds linked by a number of structural and behavioural features. The most important of these is the fully webbed foot, in which the hind toe is turned forward and connected by a web of skin to the inmost of the forward pointing toes. They are used by the birds in swimming.

The pelican dives towards water to catch its food.

Mute swans

Swans, Geese and Ducks

Swans, geese and ducks form one of the most successful and widespread groups of water birds and are found throughout the world in all sorts of freshwater habitats from small pools and ditches to large lakes or torrential streams. Many species have taken to a marine life and although they never occur as truly oceanic birds, they are found around coasts and in estuaries of all sorts. Features which they all share include their short legs and large webbed feet, long necks, and heads adorned with a big flattened bill. Easily recognised as members of their order, many species are familiar domestic or ornamental birds.

For part at least of their lives most of these birds are social species, forming in wintertime huge flocks, in which family groups may remain united. Swans will protect their territory fiercely when breeding; but geese and ducks often nest together. The young are ready to take to the water as soon as they hatch. At this time the adults moult, but unlike other birds in which the flight feathers are shed singly, they lose all the primaries at once, so they are unable to fly. This period of eclipse, when any distinctive breeding plumage is also lost, is one at which the birds normally keep to the water away from enemies as much as possible.

Swans are the largest and most clearly defined members of the group. All are large, with very long necks, which they dip into water when taking their mainly plant food. They are found throughout the world and most species are pure white in colour, although there is a black-necked swan from South America and a completely black swan from Australia. They are among the heaviest of flying birds and have difficulty in taking off, running across the water for a considerable distance before becoming airborne. Their strong, slow wing beats produce a loud whistling noise, quite unlike the flight sound of any other birds.

Types of Geese

Geese are more varied in size and appearance. The five species of grey geese, from one of which the main domestic species is descended, are to be found mostly in the Old World, while the white geese are chiefly New World in distribution. Black geese are found in both hemispheres and one species, the Canada goose is now becoming a common sight in Europe, where it has been imported as an

The dabbling ducks include the teal, which is the smallest among them, the mallard, the pintail, which is probably the most numerous duck in the world, and the shoveler, with its curiously shaped bill. The diving ducks include the tufted duck and the pochard. Eiders are sea ducks, feeding on sea urchins and crustaceans, while scoters, harlequins, goldeneyes and goosanders belong to a rather variable group which are all good divers. The ruddy duck and the white-headed duck are expert swimmers on inland waters. There are also shelducks and perching ducks.

ornamental bird, but continues to thrive when it escapes from domestication. When geese migrate from their sub-arctic breeding grounds, their wings make less noise in flight than those of swans. Many, especially those that migrate at night, call to each other in flight and can be heard over quite long distances. Like swans, geese are plant feeders, grazing on waterside pastures or stubble fields.

Duck Species

Ducks are the most numerous and varied of the group. Some, such as the shelduck are goose-like in size and appearance; others, such as the teals, are tiny with shorter necks than any geese. They tend to be more brightly coloured than swans or geese, and have a bright bar, the speculum, in the wing. Dabbling ducks, which are probably the best known species, are widespread surface swimmers, up-ending for their plant food. These birds are capable of springing directly from the water into flight.

Diving ducks, a group which again include many common species, are capable of swimming under water in their search for food, but they cannot take off without pattering across the water for some distance. Eiders are marine ducks, best known for the habit of the female of preening out her down feathers to line her nest. Other diving ducks also feed on sea urchins and molluscs, but the mergansers and their relatives have become specialised fish-eaters, with narrow, saw-edged bills for holding their slippery prey. The stiff-tailed ducks are also very good swimmers, but are found mainly in freshwater areas. These birds probably use their long, stiff tail feathers as underwater rudders.

One of the most important gods of ancient Egypt was Thoth, the god of intelligence and wisdom, and scribe to other gods. He is always represented as having the head of an ibis, and it may well be that the questing, alert look of the sacred ibis searching for food was the inspiration for this image.

Flamingos

Strangest of all, however, are the perching ducks, a group which includes many rather large birds, often referred to as geese. These birds, in spite of their webbed feet, are forest species and often perch and nest in trees. A number of species of ducks from several of the sub-groups have been domesticated, but the untamed kinds form a considerable wildfowl resource and many efforts have been made to conserve them.

Herons and Flamingos

The heron-like birds are another worldwide group of waterfowl, usually large in size, with long legs, long necks and long bills. Their food varies from one species to another. Herons and bitterns catch fishes and other small vertebrates in their long beaks. Larger invertebrates are the major food of the ibises and small water organisms are eaten by the spoonbills. A heron often stands motionless in shallow water until, perhaps, its long legs are mistaken for the stems of water plants by an unwary fish. The stillness of the heron is deceptive, for in a flash the fish is caught in its long beak, and quickly swallowed.

Some tropical species of heron stalk quietly through the water with their wings spread to cast a shadow, so that the bird can see more easily into the water. The heron's equipment for fish feeding includes powder down—a special structure of some of the feathers, which breaks down to make a substance like French chalk—and a comb-like structure on one of the toes. These two adaptations enable the bird to clean its plumage of the slime which might otherwise damage it.

Storks are large relatives of the herons. They are usually less aquatic in their way of life and in Europe the white stork, which often builds its bulky nests on chimney tops, is regarded as a symbol of good luck.

Flamingos are among the strangest looking of birds, yet their extremely long legs and necks and curiously heavy-billed heads all have a purpose in their way of life. They feed on the microscopic life suspended in the usually brackish or salty water near which they live. They wade into the

Cranes in flight

African crowned crane

shallows and twist their necks so that the deeply ridged upper part of the bill is upside down in the water. Water currents are forced through the partly open beak by the tongue, which acts as a piston, and the minute animal life is strained out by close-set horny flaps attached to the roof of the mouth. This mechanism must be very efficient, for the salt or alkaline water of the feeding places of the birds would be poisonous if taken in large quantities. The bright pink colour of the flamingos depends to some extent on the type of food which they eat. In captivity they may become paler unless special additives are included in their diet.

Cranes

Bearing a superficial likeness to the herons and storks, although not in fact closely related to them are the cranes. These large birds, with their long necks and heads, generally live in marshy areas, feeding on a wide variety of insects and small invertebrates. In flight they may be distinguished from similar birds by their outstretched necks, which are not carried tucked into the shoulders as in herons and storks. Some kinds of cranes migrate long distances between their breeding and wintering grounds. The whooping crane, one of the world's rarest birds, breeds in Alaska and migrates to the southern United States. Although many species of crane are recorded as flying at great height while on migration, they are easy prey for hunters and several species have been brought to the edge of extinction.

Cranes have spectacular courtship displays in which a number of birds dance and bow, flying up a few feet into the air, as if jerked on invisible strings. Cranes normally mate for life, usually rearing two young each year in nests which may be little more than a scrape in the open ground. Although not brightly coloured, apart from bright red skin round the face in some species, cranes have figured largely in oriental art. The crowned crane, with its attractive tuft of feathers on top of its head, is the national bird of Uganda, where it is valued, among other things, for the numbers of harmful insects and small vertebrates which it destroys.

Related to the cranes, and far less spectacular in size and behaviour although more numerous in species, are the rails and the crakes. These smallish, secretive birds, usually camouflaged in delicate shades of brown, hide in hedgerows or reed beds and may be very difficult to see. Some of the more obvious members of the group have taken to an aquatic life. In temperate latitudes flocks of moorhens and coots may be a common sight. The coots have lobed feet like the grebes; moorhens have only long, thin unwebbed toes. As they swim, their heads bob forward with each stroke, making it look as if life in water is a great effort for them.

The Waders

A large number of water birds, usually lumped together as waders, may be divided into the sandpipers and the plovers. The sandpipers are in general northern species. They are essentially birds of seashore and estuary where they make a living from the small worms and crustaceans

Herring gull

below the surface of the mud. Their large feet support them over the softest of surfaces, their long legs enable them to wade into shallow water and their long necks and bills enable them to probe for their food.

The plovers, which in general have a more southerly distribution, and in many cases are found in more inland sites than the sandpipers, have usually a more compact form, and shorter beaks. Most waders migrate great distances between their breeding places, which are chiefly in areas of high moor and tundra, to the unfrozen estuaries and mudflats where they spend the winter. Great flocks migrate down the coastal flyways, feeding, resting and preening in suitably remote and undisturbed spots. One of the most amazing sights for the winter birdwatcher is to see a flock of perhaps 10,000 small waders take off and wheel through the air with military precision, every bird keeping station in relation to its nearest neighbours and the whole flock moving as one.

Waders nest on the ground, usually laying four pointed eggs which fit snugly with the narrow end inwards into the slight hollow where they are laid. The eggs are normally very well camouflaged and difficult to see, as is the incubating bird, for most waders' plumage is in shades of brown and grey which blend perfectly with their moorland home. A few species are black and white but these are mostly beach-nesters, so the abrupt patches of colour break up their outline and disguise them among the pebbles. The young are quickly independent of their parents and although in the first hours they look as if their outsize legs lead a life of their own unconnected to the rest of the body, they are soon running and feeding.

Gulls, Terns and Skuas

Gulls to many people are the most obvious birds of the sea. Strangely, though, they are creatures of the beach and inshore waters, and most of them never venture over the open oceans. Indeed, some gulls breed on inland marshes or lakes and never see the sea. A few kinds are becoming town birds: the black-headed gull, for instance, vies with the pigeons for food in many European cities, although it is far from being as confiding as the true land birds. The only oceanic gull in Europe is the kittiwake, a migratory bird which comes to the coasts of the north Atlantic to nest on sheer cliffs beyond the reach of predators.

The king vulture, which comes from Mexico, has a naked head with brilliantly coloured beak and neck and a warted appearance. It is one of the New World vultures, or condors, which differ in many respects from Old World vultures.

Parakeets are members of the parrot family and live in America. They have colourful plumage and a beak typical of the group. Below is another tropical bird, the anhinga, also from America, and a member of the gull family, a black skimmer.

Great black-backed gull

Also highly oceanic are the terns. These long-winged, fork-tailed birds are sometimes called sea swallows, but their delicate appearance is misleading, for they can weather storms at sea and the longest-distance migrant of all birds is found among them. Nesting in noisy colonies on the edge of the beach, terns are among the most vulnerable of sea birds to disturbance.

The skuas are another group related to the gulls. These are among the pirates of the seas, for they rarely hunt for themselves but prefer to rob other birds of their catch. These large, brown, long-tailed birds seem to know when another bird is carrying fish in its crop—perhaps from its way of flight. They harry the hunter until in desperation, and perhaps to lighten itself for escape from the aggressor, the unfortunate bird drops its prey. Before the fish has hit the water it is scooped out of the air by the skua, which in spite of its size is very agile in flight. The appearance of a skua often seems to terrify other sea birds, especially terns.

Auks, which are short-winged, dark-coloured sea birds, are also related to the gulls. They spend almost the whole of their life at sea swimming and diving for their food. They are a further demonstration of the adaptability of this great group to a variety of marine environments.

Birds of Prey

Many kinds of birds feed on flesh, but two groups—the birds of prey and the owls—have become highly specialised in a hunting way of life, and feed mainly on the higher vertebrates. Both are usually brown-coloured birds, found on all the continents except Antarctica. Both kill their prey with their strong, sharp talons and pluck and tear the flesh with their narrow, hooked beaks. These birds normally swallow huge chunks of food and regurgitate pellets of indigestible matter.

However, there are many differences as well, for the two groups are not closely related. The similarities reflect a similar way of life. They can exist in the same area together since they are active at different times, the birds of prey during daylight hours and the owls at night. Owls' plumage, even the primary feathers, is soft, to reduce the noise of their wing-beats. Although their eyesight is excellent and adapted to make the best use of poor light, they also have a highly developed sense of hearing. Under experimental conditions it was discovered that a barn owl could catch its prey in total darkness, using its ears to judge the distance perfectly.

Types of Nest

Owls usually nest in holes, laying white eggs, which may be numerous when food is plentiful. Birds of prey normally make a nest of sticks, grass and mosses and lay a small clutch of brown blotched eggs. Both types of bird begin incubation with the laying of the first egg so that the young birds hatch on different days. The first chicks are bigger and stronger than the later members of the brood.

Owls, as a group, tend to be alike, but the birds of prey vary greatly in many respects. The smallest is the Philippine falconet, which is only about 6 centimetres (6 inches) long and eats insects; the largest is the Andean condor, with a wing-span of nearly three metres (ten feet), which feeds mainly on carrion. Some birds of prey are fast fliers; others soar or hover when looking for their food.

Standing apart from the group as a whole is the secretary bird of Africa. It gets its name from the long, drooping head-feathers which look like quill pens stuck behind the ears of a Dickensian clerk or secretary. It is a strong-legged bird which walks with long, stately strides. It feeds on large insects, reptiles, rodents and ground nesting birds. To kill its prey it kicks with its powerful feet. Because of its value as a destroyer of pests, it is protected over much of its range.

Vultures

Vultures are found in the warmer parts of both the Old and New Worlds. In spite of many similarities in appearance, the various species are very distantly related and have developed separately for a very long time. Vultures are all large birds, with huge, oblong wings, finger-like at the tips to control air flow during soaring flight. In spite of their size, vultures have relatively weak beaks and their talons are straight and unsuited for killing or rending. But their food is entirely carrion, often taken, as in the case of the Egyptian vulture, in a very rotten state. They use thermal air currents to soar to great heights, where they survey the ground for possible food. Any bird flying down at the sight of food will be seen by birds patrolling adjacent beats and they will follow. The result is that any dead animal is quickly surrounded by vultures which may have come to the feast from several miles away. They perform a valuable service, along with other scavengers, in removing carcasses which would otherwise rot and become a health hazard.

The rest of the birds of prey are active hunters, but their methods vary considerably. The eagles, which are powerful soaring birds, live mainly in open country and mountains,

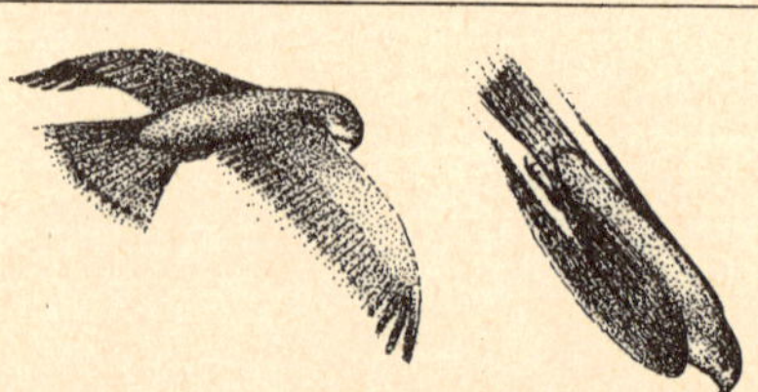

Birds of prey attack in two ways. The kestrel, on the left, hovers over its prey before descending feet first. The falcon, on the right, "stoops" or dives head first at its prey. Both catch the prey in their talons.

Egyptian vulture

Falconry, the art of catching game with birds of prey, was first practised in the Far East before 1000 B.C. Introduced into Europe in the ninth century it was, until the invention of guns for shooting birds, the chief sport of the aristocracy. Almost all sorts of birds of prey have been used, from eagles to male sparrowhawks. The birds to be used for falconry must be taken from the nest shortly before they are able to fly. Taming the falcon is a job requiring skill and dedication and since the bird needs to be flown fairly frequently, should only be attempted by someone with plenty of time to give to it. The trained bird wears a hood which covers its eyes and prevents it from becoming frightened by strange sights and sounds, but can be removed very quickly if it is to be flown. At all times the hawk carries small bells on its legs. These enable the falconer to hear where the bird is if it hides in dense trees while being flown, and to keep an ear on its welfare while the bird is confined in its cage, which is called a mew.

Golden eagle swooping on its prey

although the largest of all, the harpy eagle of South America and the monkey-eating eagle of the Philippines are both forest-dwellers. Their large size often makes their movements look slow, but the speed of their attack as they stoop on their prey is as fast as any movement in the bird world.

They feed on a wide variety of animals; the golden eagle hunts mainly rabbits, mountain hares, grouse and very occasionally a sickly lamb. The buzzards, which are also soaring birds and are related to the true hawks, are a good deal smaller than eagles. They have much weaker beaks and feet and only tackle smaller prey. The fish eagles are large birds of prey which haunt lakes and rivers and the edge of the sea for their prey. The osprey is also a fish-eater, diving into the water to capture its prey with its talons. Kites, generally recognisable by their forked tails are often scavengers. Indeed in some parts of the world they are the most obvious birds of prey.

The true hawks are broad-winged, long-tailed birds, adapted to life in woodlands where they stalk and pounce on their prey, which consists mainly of small birds, although mammals and reptiles are also taken. The most spectacular of the birds of prey are the falcons. These vary from tiny species no bigger than a thrush to the gyrfalcon, which is 55 centimetres (22 inches) long. All falcons have long, pointed wings, and are capable of tremendous speed when stooping on their prey. They hunt mainly other birds, which they strike down in flight, normally breaking the back with a blow of their half-closed talons, catching their victim before it flutters to the ground.

Because of their gracefully controlled flight and their apparent courage, the birds of prey have always appealed to man. But man has always feared for his flocks and his stock in their presence and so has tended to destroy the birds whenever possible. This destruction reached its zenith in Britain at the end of the last century, when one species of bird of prey, the osprey, was completely wiped out and several others were reduced to a very low level. Now, when few people wish them harm, the flesh-eating birds are under a greater threat than ever before. Throughout the world they are being destroyed by the remains of chemical pest-killers in their food; the build-up in their tissues means that they cannot reproduce and eventually they die.

Tropical Birds

Grouped under this popular heading are nine orders of birds which include some of the most colourful and unusual species. The term 'tropical' has no exact meaning as used here. It is merely a convenient banner under which to list those birds, like parrots, which have come to represent for the people of northern Europe all the exotic qualities of tropical lands.

Parrots

No group of birds contains more colourful creatures than the parrots and their allies. Their names alone have a fascinating sound—parakeets, macaws, cockatoos, budgerigars. They come in all sizes, from the tiny pygmy parrots of New Guinea to the big spectacular macaws which live in the Amazon forests. A distinguishing feature is the shape of their beaks, short and strongly hooked with the upper part hanging far over the lower. Nearly all of them use this hooked beak to help them climb.

Parrots have always been popular pets, because they behave at times almost like humans, holding food in their feet as if they were hands and 'talking' to their owners. This ability to 'speak' is purely imitative and can only be learned in captivity. The greatest talker of them all is the African grey parrot, which has been taught to imitate the sound of the human voice since the days of ancient Greece and Rome.

The cockatoos are large, crested birds with beautiful plumage, and the parakeets include the most popular of all caged birds, the budgerigar.

Swifts

Among the most interesting things about the swift family are the nests some of them make, partly or wholly, from saliva. This is a stringy fluid, rather like a thick solution of gum which forms in the mouth of the bird and when exposed to the air rapidly dries and hardens.

Many animals make use of saliva as a means of binding together materials during building operations but the edible swift of eastern Asia and the Pacific islands is unique in providing man with birds' nest soup, regarded as a great delicacy, particularly in China. This is made from the nests themselves, the most favoured ones being white-coloured and built entirely of saliva, which are gathered from the caves where the bird lives.

Another extraordinary nest is made by one of the scissor-tailed swifts of Central America. This is a great hanging tube over half a metre (two feet) long and 150 millimetres (six inches) across, with an opening at the lower end for the birds to pass in and out.

Apart from nest-building the swifts' greatest distinction is their flying skill. No other bird can rival the swift of eastern Asia for speed and agility. It lives entirely on insects taken in flight, which it swoops down on and catches at speeds of over 160 kilometres (100 miles) per hour.

Allied to the swifts but distinctive because of their smallness and brilliant, multi-coloured plumage are the humming birds. They feed from the nectar of flowers, which they gather while hovering in the air. The incredibly fast beat of their wings as they hover produces the humming sound which gives them their name. The wings move so quickly that they seem to be almost invisible. There are over 300 species, mostly in South and Central America.

Trogons

If a choice had to be made of the typical tropical bird it might well be the male quetzal, one of the trogons, with its bright metallic colours and remarkably long tail plumes.

All trogons are striking, multi-hued birds and their distribution through three continents (South America, Africa and Asia) has proved something of a puzzle to scientists, for the trogon is a home-loving bird and hardly ever leaves its immediate area. Although the various species probably come from a common stock no one can be sure where they originated. The discovery of fossil remains of a trogon-type bird in rock strata dating back some thirty million years suggests that the present-day birds may be survivors of a very ancient group. All species live almost entirely on fruits and berries.

The quetzal gave its name to Quetzalcoatl, the chief god of the Toltecs. Its feathers, plucked from living birds, were used by the Aztecs and Mayas to make ceremonial helmets.

Kingfishers

It is one of the unexpected results of scientific classification to discover that the exquisite, darting kingfisher is placed in the same group of birds

Amazon parrot

Gold and blue macaw

as the great hornbill of south-east Asia, which can be over one and a half metres (five feet) long. Yet both have a particular body structure which relates them to each other.

Typical of the many species of kingfisher which are found in every part of the world is the common kingfisher, which decorates the shores of rivers and lakes in northern Europe, Asia and North Africa. It belongs to the group of fishing kingfishers which live on small fishes taken from the water. This tiny bird skims over the water to take its place on an overhanging bough of a tree. Here it will wait motionless until it marks out its prey. Then it darts like a flash into the water to take a fish in its long pointed bill.

Common in Australia is the kookaburra, or laughing jackass, which belongs to the kingfisher family and gets its name from its weird cry.

The hornbill uses its great beak partly as a defence weapon but chiefly to serve as a trowel for plastering up the holes in trees in which the female nests. These holes are found high up in the trunks of straight trees. When the female is safely settled inside, the male plasters up the opening with mud, leaving a tiny hole in the centre through which its mate can be fed.

Pigeons

There are pigeons all over the world and many of them are very decorative, such as the gay blue-crowned pigeon from New Guinea. More familiar in the Old World is the rock dove and in North America the mourning dove.

Fancy domestic pigeons and the homing pigeons kept for racing are probably descended from the rock dove, so too are the flocks of semi-tame pigeons which live in and around buildings in European cities in such great numbers that they create something of a nuisance. Rock doves and their descendants are very sociable birds, living in large flocks, eating, sleeping and moving about in unison.

Another group in the family are the fruit pigeons, so called because they

The kookaburra, or laughing jackass, of Australia belongs to a family of forest kingfishers. Its nickname comes from its weird cries, like a chorus of wild human laughter.

Common kingfisher

feed mainly on fruits and berries, especially wild nutmegs which they swallow whole.

There is no real technical difference between the use of the names pigeon and dove, although the larger birds are usually called pigeons and the smaller ones doves. Carrier or homing pigeons are not a separate breed but are the result of cross-breeding, controlled by man in his efforts to obtain a highly developed sense of direction and homing instinct.

Cuckoos

The call of the male cuckoo in springtime as it sings to its mate is possibly the best-known bird sound in the Old World. The common cuckoo spreads its cry over most parts of Europe and Asia and its name has found its way into many languages in words that imitate its call. The other very familiar thing about the cuckoo is the fact that it has the habit of laying its eggs in other birds' nests.

But the common cuckoo of Eurasia is only one of over a hundred cuckoo species which range from the emerald cuckoo of Africa to the stout-legged roadrunner which lives on the ground in the deserts of America. It is a very fast runner, feeds on snakes and lizards, but makes only a feeble effort at flying.

The dodo is an extinct bird, very heavily built and quite unable to fly. It belonged to a small family of birds confined to the islands of Mauritius, Réunion and Rodriguez in the Indian Ocean. It had a large, hooked beak, short stubby legs and rudimentary wings. Clumsy and defenceless, the dodo was an easy prey to the sailors who landed on the islands in the seventeenth century. Those birds which were not destroyed by human hand were attacked by other animals introduced by man to the islands. The appearance of the dodo is known today from contemporary drawings, from relics of stuffed specimens and from remains of skeletons dug up on the islands.

Woodpeckers

Members of the woodpecker family spend their lives in trees, and wherever there is a forest the woodpecker will thrive. They have distinctive bills, straight and pointed for digging into the bark of trees. They also have very long tongues which can be thrust out a great distance to grub out from holes and crevices the hidden insect life on which they feed.

Perching Birds

Although many birds belonging to a number of orders are capable of perching, the members of one group, which includes over half of all known birds, are referred to as the perching birds. They are the common birds of garden and woodland, for they are all land-living and found throughout the world, except for Antarctica. They always have four strong, unwebbed toes, with the hind toe always well developed. Most perching birds have tuneful voices and song is an important part of their life, being used for territorial definition and—as call notes—for communication. Mimicry of other sounds occurs as part of some songs. The lyre bird, for example, will include snatches of all sorts of sounds in its song and it is well known that in many species the song has to be learned and may be modified in the process.

Perching birds vary in size from the raven, which is about 66 centimetres (26 inches) long to some of the tiny wrens and kinglets, which are about 8 centimetres (3 inches) long. Their colours vary from dull browns and blacks to vividly blotched patterns on some of the finches. Their food includes insects of all sorts, taken by bills well suited for the job—fine forceps for the smaller insects and coarser pincers for the bigger kinds. Some feed on buds, leaves or seeds. Those which feed on smaller types of food have short, stubby beaks and those which eat larger and tougher fruits have strong, conical beaks. The hawfinch, which can crack cherry and olive stones with ease, has such a beak.

All perching birds produce young which are naked, blind and helpless at birth and are tended for a period of at least two weeks in a well-constructed nest. Most nests are

Young cuckoo being fed by a female whitethroat

built in trees, well away from the ground, some in thickety branches like that of the blackbird and some hanging from a twig like the goldcrests. Blackbirds incorporate a foundation of mud into their nests; swallows and their relatives make mud the major material of the nest. In common with other perching birds, the swallow's nursery is furnished with a warm lining of hair, feathers, grass or moss. Some breed singly in a strongly defended territory, like robins. Others, like rooks, are social nesters, which may burden a single tree with twenty of their big, stick-based nests. African weaver birds band together in hundreds, their finely woven nests looking like strange fruits hanging abundantly from the branches of their chosen trees.

Egg-laying

That such highly evolved animals as birds should have retained the old-fashioned, reptilian method of reproduction by laying eggs may at first seem surprising. But the system as adapted by the birds, is in fact ideal, for it enables the female to produce a large brood without overburdening herself. The eggs in most species are laid daily and incubation does not start until the clutch is complete. Initial cooling does not harm the embryo; cooling after development has started is quickly fatal. Eggs vary in shape from nearly round to long and oval, although most are more strongly pointed at one end than the other. Colours vary from white, which is usual in hole nesters, to blues and browns and eggs spotted in various shades, which are the masterpieces of camouflage laid by ground nesters.

Perching birds are popular with most human beings because of their bright colours, their cheerful songs and their often comical display antics in the breeding season. In some parts of the world certain species have become pests of crops, but in general they are in more danger from man's wish to collect them to keep as pets, than from persecution because of any damage they may do. Some kinds of tropical finch are collected for sale all over the world, the duller coloured species having their colours heightened by being dyed bright pink or green. In some countries it is illegal

There is an astonishing variety of nests made by the different species of birds in which to raise their young. Nests seen here are: blackbird (left), goldcrest (below), swallow (right) and those in a rookery.

Birds' eggs belonging to 1 rook, 2 magpie, 3 jackdaw, 4 bullfinch, 5 yellowhammer, 6 chaffinch, 7 song thrush, 8 blackbird, 9 mistlethrush, 10 puffin, 11 guillemot, 12 partridge, 13 nightjar, 14 corncrake, 15 great tit, 16 nuthatch, 17 blue tit, 18 robin, 19 nightingale, 20 swallow.

to keep wild birds caged; but many people have the pleasure of birds' company by encouraging them in gardens and getting them to visit bird tables.

The provision of food, water and shelter will attract birds to a garden. The food can be in the form of berry-bearing plants, or a bird table furnished with nuts, fat, bread and other food enjoyed by garden birds. A bird table will be better patronised if it is placed near to some cover from which the birds can survey the situation and to which they can escape quickly if necessary. Water is a necessity both for drinking and for bathing, and cover can be provided in the form of thick bushes or hedges, supplemented by nest boxes in the breeding season.

Bird Tables

Even the commonest garden birds are attractive. In hard weather they will parade at a bird table and may be seen at close quarters. The thrushes include the small song thrush and its larger, greyer cousin, the mistle thrush. This bird is sometimes called the storm cock, for it starts to sing its fine territorial song in mid-winter and can often be heard, even in very rough weather, as it announces its early bid for nesting space. The blackbird, which is black in the male, with a bright yellow beak, but dark brown in the female, is a relative of the thrushes.

All of these birds may be seen tug-of-warring with worms on a lawn. The song thrush will catch snails and smash them open on a favourite anvil stone. Starlings are basically black birds, speckled with a 'milky way' of small spots, from which they get their name. The male has a fine green gloss to his feathers in springtime and it is then that he is most vocal, singing his curious, squeaky song, and giving imitations of other birds' sounds. Sparrows, which were common town birds until horses were replaced by motor transport, can still be seen in gardens. They squabble and dustbath and sunbathe, and through most of the summer build their untidy nests in any crevice into which they can squeeze. Finches include the greenfinch, in which the male is a handsome yellowish green, although his mate is less brightly coloured.

Male chaffinches are among the most colourful of garden birds, with rosy pink breasts and blue-grey heads, but again their mates are less attractive. Also very brightly coloured are bullfinches, which may invade suburban gardens. These are not always welcome, however, because of their habit of stripping ornamental shrubs or fruit trees of their buds, which does not endear them to most gardeners. Titmice are common bird table visitors. The tiny blue tit and its larger cousin the great tit are the

commonest visitors and give pleasure to many people with their acrobatic behaviour. Another acrobatic visitor to bird tables is the nuthatch. This bird has strong curved toes, which enable it to climb vertical and overhanging surfaces with ease.

The Robin

One of the most confiding birds of gardens is the robin who will quickly discover and exploit any food supply which is provided. It can become very tame, even to the extent of tapping on windows and demanding food when none is available outside. In some cases it will even enter houses. The robin is an enterprising and quick little bird, and with its bright appearance and cheerful song it has endeared itself to many people.

Common garden birds seen here are, from left to right, song thrush, starling, female and male chaffinch, male house sparrow (behind) great tit (top), nuthatch (centre), blue tit (below), male house sparrow and, from top to bottom, male blackbird, robin, male greenfinch and female house sparrow.

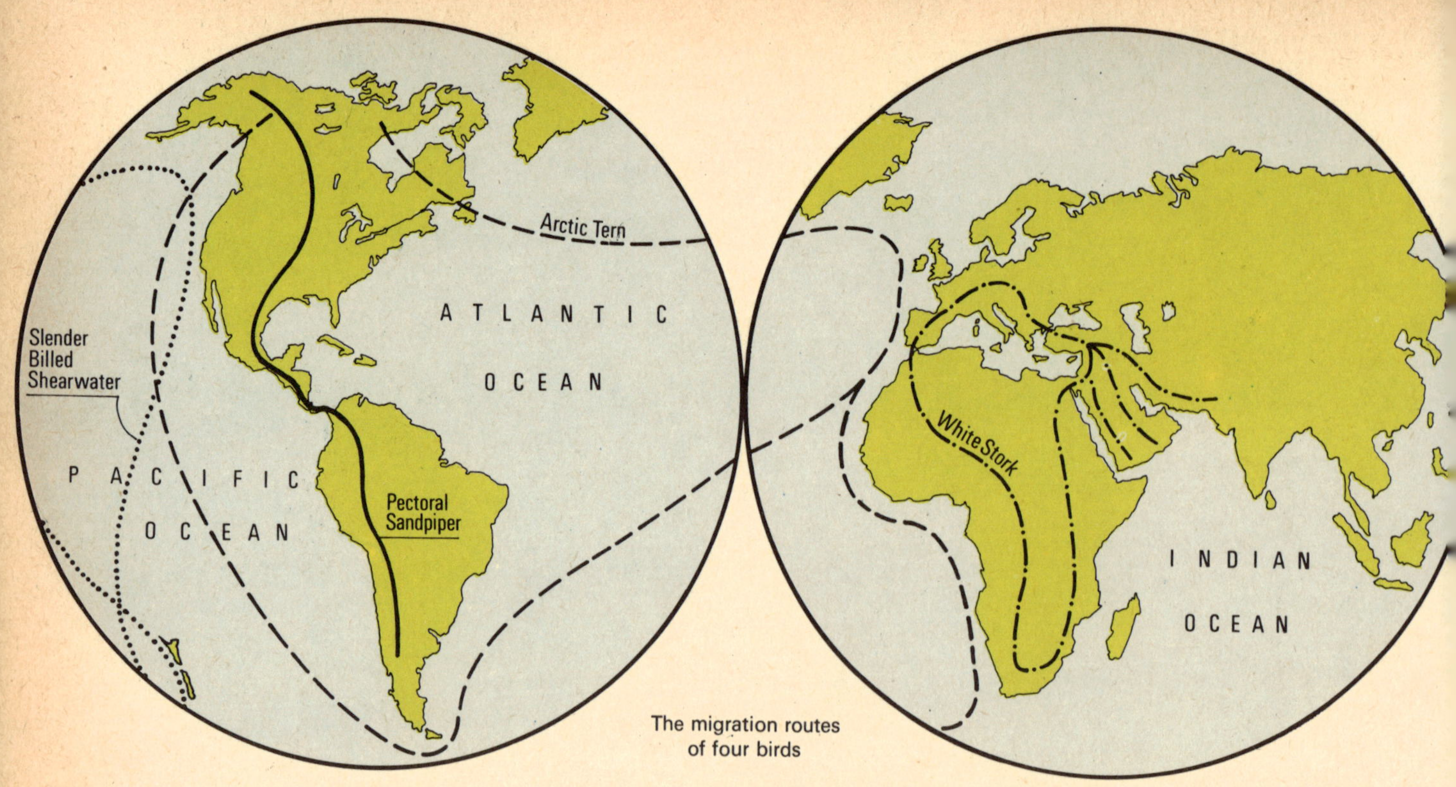

The migration routes of four birds

Bird Migration

One of the mysteries about birds, observed since Old Testament times but not explained until recently, is the fact that they are in many cases not permanent residents of any given area. At a certain time of year flocks will arrive, to disappear again a few months later. Only in modern times have the scale and scope of these migratory movements been realised. For many of the birds concerned are tiny and for long it was thought impossible that they should make journeys which are often tens of thousands of kilometres, involving long sea crossings.

Many birds die on these journeys, especially the smaller ones, yet the advantages must outweigh the difficulties and dangers, for migration is the habit of many species. Some birds migrate in large flocks, some in family parties and some singly. In a few cases the distances are short and may merely involve movement in level rather than latitude.

Migration Routes

In general the routes chosen tend to follow sea coasts, valleys and other landmarks which make a pattern of traditional flyways. The knowledge of these is inborn in many species but experiments have shown that in some cases, at least, the birds are able to navigate, using the sun and stars, and are able to correct their position if they are artificially displaced. Migration is normally in a northerly direction in the early part of the year, with a return south in later months. The reason for this is probably that the huge land masses of the northern continents offer space for breeding and longer daylight hours in which to collect food for the brood than would be available in the tropics.

The longest-distance traveller among migrant birds is the Arctic tern, which breeds in coastal and offshore areas of the northern hemisphere, but spends the winter months in the Antarctic, making a round trip of about 35,000 kilometres (22,000 miles) each year. Some other sea birds also make immense journeys. The slender-billed shearwater, which nests on the coasts of South Australia, migrates across the Pacific Ocean to the west coast of America. Then, making a second more northerly ocean crossing, it completes the circle back to its nesting place by the next year.

Land birds may make journeys which are scarcely less great. The pectoral sandpiper is an American bird, nesting in the far north of the continent and migrating south in the winter time, paralleling the movements made by European and Asiatic waders.

Not all the members of a population migrate in the same direction when the time comes to leave the breeding grounds. The white storks of Europe travel over two distinct routes, those from the more westerly parts taking a western coastal route, those from eastern Europe taking a line south-east to fly over the lands which border the eastern side of the Mediterranean.

Movements during migration are traced by attaching metal rings to a bird's leg or by marking them with a harmless dye.

Tracing Bird Movement

Our knowledge of migration comes in a variety of ways. Observation was the first and is still used, sometimes to note the arrival and departure times of the birds, sometimes to track them on their journeys. Birds may be trapped in a number of harmless ways and banded with lightweight numbered metal rings. Later, recoveries—in traps on other migration journeys or after death—show the distance the bird has travelled. Hundreds of thousands of birds are banded each year. The percentage of recoveries is small, but enough over the years to have built up a complex picture of the long-distance movements of birds.

Mammals

To the majority of people, mammals are the most familiar animals. They are to be found almost everywhere: from the edge of the Arctic ice sheets to the tropics; from the sea to the driest deserts; from the tops of trees to below the ground. They range in size from the blue whale, which may be over thirty metres (100 feet) long and weigh more than 120 tons, to the pygmy shrews which are less than 50 millimetres (two inches) long and weigh only about seven grammes (a quarter of an ounce). Mammals may feed on meat, on insects, or on many kinds of vegetation. Some, like pigs or man, will eat almost any kind of food. Between them, mammals use to the full the area in which they live.

Varieties of Mammals

What are the qualities which make an animal a mammal? Appearances are nothing to go by, for mammals may have long legs like antelopes, or no legs like sea cows. They may have long necks like giraffes, or very short ones like elephants. They may have shaggy coats like bears, or smooth skins like whales. They may be a variety of colours, spotted, striped or blotched. Yet all are backboned animals, breathing air and warm-blooded. Most important of all, in most cases the young are born at a relatively advanced stage and they are always cared for and fed on milk by their mothers. No other kinds of creatures give this sort of protection and feeding to their young and it accounts, in large part, for the success of the mammals.

Mammals are physically efficient animals. Their constant temperature (which is what is meant by the term 'warm-blooded') means that the chemical activity of the cells of their bodies can proceed at a steady rate, regardless of outside conditions. Because of this they are able to be continuously active, even in cold weather, and can live in cool parts of the world. Their turnover of energy is rapid and mammals begin the digestion of their food as soon as it is taken into the mouth. Sliced or chewed with teeth specialised for the purpose and with saliva and other digestive juices added, food is quickly converted into the energy needed for life. Breathing is rapid and regular in mammals. Stale blood, with its load of body waste products, which is pumped from the heart to the lungs, is kept well separated from the blood which is returned, freshly mixed with oxygen, to be pumped round the body.

Well-developed Senses

Mammals are intelligent animals, with large and complex brains and well developed senses. The head of the baboon, for example, shows the enlarged brain case. The eyes, nose and ears are all on the head and although many animals have poor eyesight and are unable to distinguish colours, most have excellent hearing and sense of smell. The large whiskers round the snout are part of the delicate and highly developed sense of touch.

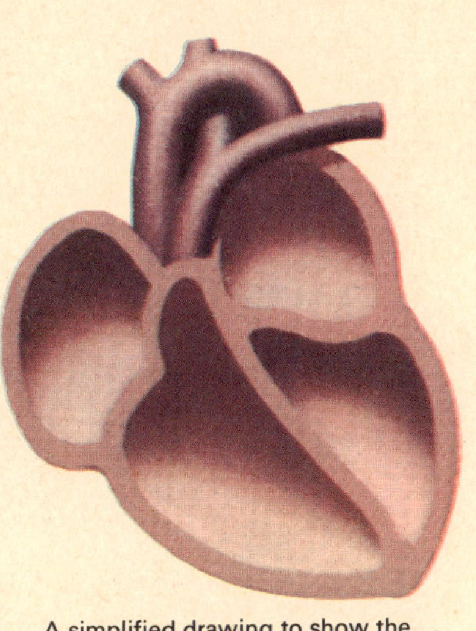

A simplified drawing to show the four-chambered heart of mammals which separates blood returning to the lungs from blood about to be pumped around the body.

All mammals share a number of features. All are vertebrates; all are air-breathing and warm-blooded; all have fur or hair; and all suckle their young on milk. Mammals are active animals with skeletons which support their bodies precisely. All of them have a definite size. Their limb bones grow at the ends, which have loose sections while the animal is young, but which fuse and prevent further growth when it becomes adult. Mammal lower jaws are composed of two bones fused together which carry the teeth for cutting (incisors), tearing (canines) and chewing (molars). Mammals have special blood cells which make them more efficient carriers of oxygen. Finally, all have large and complex brains and are generally intelligent.

Primitive Mammals

The first mammals evolved from reptile ancestors about 200 million years ago. We do not know exactly what they were like, for their fossilised remains which are small and fragile are rarely found. There are however two creatures, the platypus from Australia and the spiny anteater found in Australia and New Guinea, which give us some clues. For both lay eggs, like reptiles do, although both suckle their young, like mammals. Both of these animals lead extremely specialised lives and their physical structure gives us no exact information on their ancient ancestors.

The koala is a tree-dweller and feeds on the leaves of eucalyptus trees.

Marsupials

In Australia, South America and parts of North America, other primitive mammals live. These are called marsupials, a name that comes from the Latin word for a pouch. In the marsupials the young grow for a short time in their mothers' bodies. They are very tiny and under-developed at birth—the biggest measures only 25 millimetres (one inch) long and the smaller species of marsupials produce babies which are only about the size of a grain of rice. The little creature is strong enough for one thing, which is to push its way through its mother's fur and find the pouch on her underside where the milk glands are situated. The tiny animal clamps its jaws on to a nipple and remains feeding in safety and warmth in the pouch until it has grown big and strong enough to venture out on its own, a process that may take several months. Even then, it will return to take shelter when danger threatens.

At one time marsupial animals lived in many parts of the world, but they were mostly destroyed by more efficient and cleverer animals called placental mammals, when these evolved. Few placentals reached South America and none reached Australia so in these two areas the marsupials continued to flourish.

The best known of the marsupials are the kangaroos, which are the native grazing animals of Australia. There are many other kinds of pouched mammals, fitted for different ways of life. The koala, which looks so much like a bear, is a tree-living marsupial, feeding on certain species of Australian eucalyptus. Others, such as the almost extinct thylacine, which looks like a striped dog, feed on flesh. The opossums feed on small animals and the phalangers mainly on insects. Other marsupials look like mice, or moles or monkeys, but in all cases they are pouched mammals, survivors of the prehistoric past.

Kangaroos are timid animals, living in groups called droves. Each drove usually has a particular district and feeding ground which it frequents.

The platypus is a puzzle creature. In spite of its duck-like bill it has the furry body of a typical mammal, but it cannot control its body temperature as well as most mammals and, like a reptile, may become torpid on a cold day. Strangest of all, a female platypus lays eggs. She digs a burrow in a stream bank, where she makes a nest, blocking off the main tunnel for safety. In the nest she lays her eggs which are tiny compared with the size of the adult. After being kept warm for a fortnight the eggs hatch and the tiny babies, naked and blind, nuzzle at their mother's belly and cause milk to flow, which they lap up.

The European hedgehog's food is very varied. It will eat all kinds of insects, worms, slugs, rats, mice–even snakes and lizards. It also has a special liking for birds' eggs. Here, a hedgehog is shown attacking a viper which it will kill by a series of bites.

Insect-eaters

The vast majority of mammals in the world today belong to a group called the placentals. In them, there is a special organ, the placenta, through which the unborn young are nourished and this enables them to grow to a large size before birth. They are mostly intelligent, adaptable animals and are to be found throughout the world.

The most primitive among the placentals are the insectivores. These are all small, long-snouted animals, with sharp pointed teeth for holding and slicing insects and other small prey. The fur is usually velvety although there may be spines mingled with it. There are claws on all the toes and many of the insectivores are good burrowers. The eyes and ears are often small, but the sense of touch is well developed and most insectivores have big sensory whiskers round the snout. The star-nosed mole has gone even further in this respect and has fleshy feelers on the end of its nose.

Shrews

The insectivores are physically variable and are found in many different places, almost throughout the world. Some are becoming increasingly rare, but on the whole insectivores are well able to survive in the modern world. Shrews are among the commonest of the insectivores. They are tiny, restless creatures, living anywhere that abundant prey may be found, for they need to eat their own weight daily in grubs, snails and the like to fuel their constant activity. Their tiny, shrill voices, often mistaken for insect squeaks, may be heard in the countryside at almost any time of the day or night. They sleep only briefly, for to go without food for four hours can be fatal.

The Hedgehog

The hedgehog is probably the most familiar insectivore in the Old World. Protected by its spines, which it can erect by rolling up into a ball, it shows no fear of any natural enemies. Like the shrews, the hedgehogs' need for food is constant, and they will tackle almost any small animal that they meet. Slugs, worms, insects and the eggs and even the young of ground-nesting birds fall prey to them. They are said to attack and kill adders, which exhaust themselves striking at the hedgehog's spines and cannot drive their poison home.

Hedgehogs are able to roll themselves into a compact ball for protection.

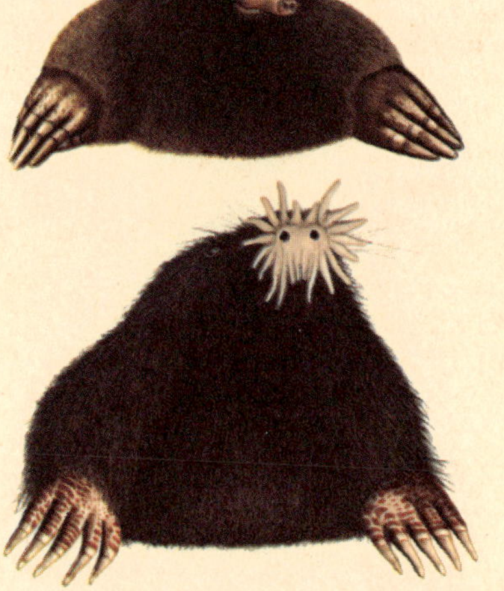

Digging is the mole's way of life. For this it uses the broad front feet, with which it first loosens the earth. Then, gripping the tunnel walls with its claws, it shoves its head and shoulders into the earth and pushes, so packing the soil firm. Sometimes the mole has to push extra soil up to the surface where it forms molehills, but when the earth is fairly loose, the mole can 'swim' below the surface. Seen above are a common mole and below it a star-nosed mole.

When food becomes scarce in the winter time, hedgehogs hibernate. They are among the mammals which have learned to live in harmony with man and many are to be found in gardens, tamed by householders who put out milk to encourage them. Hedgehogs do not, however, make good pets. Their spiny coats make grooming difficult, so they carry a zoological garden of parasites on their backs, a feature which most people find unattractive.

Moles are the expert burrowers of the insectivore world. They satisfy their enormous appetites by digging tunnels in which they catch grubs and worms to store in their nests.

Shrews produce litters of blind and toothless young which, in order to move about, form chains by holding tails.

Rodents seen below are 1 harvest mouse, 2 guinea pig, 3 brown rat, 4 prairie dog, 5 beaver, 6 lemming, 7 house mouse, 8 capybara, 9 red squirrel, 10 coypu, 11 porcupine.

Rodents

Of all the mammals, by far the largest number of kinds are included among the gnawing mammals, or rodents. These creatures have found a way to live in every environment except the sea and are to be found as runners, burrowers, climbers, gliders or swimmers throughout the world, except in Australia. Most rodents are small, the giant among them being the capybara, which is the size of a half-grown pig. In spite of variations in appearance, all rodents have many things in common. Some of these may be seen in the skull, which is long and low, with a relatively small brain case. The area for the attachment of chewing muscles is, however, great and there are pulley-like muscles running from the skull to the lower jaw which enable them to feed on very tough plant food.

The teeth are always clearly divided into the incisors in the front of the mouth and, separated by a long gap, the molars at the back. There are only two incisors in either jaw, but they are extremely powerful tools, with roots which run back into the skull. The ends of the roots are open, which means that the tooth may receive nutriment and grow throughout the life of the animal. As it chews, the teeth work against each other and get worn down, but the open roots ensure that growth keeps pace with wear, so the rodents always have serviceable nibbling teeth. Rodent incisors have a very thick layer of enamel on one side only and the cutting edge is of this very hard material, ground by wear to razor sharpness.

Enemies of Rodents

Rodents are mainly small and defenceless animals. They are the main food of many kinds of flesh-eaters, including snakes, birds of prey and mammals. That they manage to survive is due in many cases to their huge capacity for reproduction. Many of the smaller rodents may live for only one year, but in that time may produce forty or more offspring. Most of the young do not survive their early months, but normally enough do so to preserve the species. In a few kinds of rodents, however, it sometimes happens that larger than average numbers of young manage to survive the season of their birth. The following summer they

The skull of a typical rodent

become part of the breeding population and overall numbers rise accordingly, with more young again surviving. If this trend continues without being broken by exceptionally hard winters, or some other reason, numbers will build up to 'plague' proportions in a very few years.

In lemmings this seems to happen quite regularly, and the animals, under the huge pressure of their population explosion, try to migrate to new, less crowded areas. Large numbers of them move across the land, swimming rivers and lakes and sometimes even attempting to swim the sea. Some may find new quarters but most die. In the original areas of the plague the remaining population breeds at a reduced rate, due apparently to internal changes in their bodies because of the stress of constant competition.

A few kinds of rodents breed slowly. Beavers, for example, produce only one litter each spring and the young remain with their parents for two years. Beavers are long-lived animals, often surviving for twenty years.

Three Main Groups

Because of differences in their anatomies, rodents are often divided into three main groups, those of the squirrels, mice and porcupines. The squirrel group are mainly climbers, with long claws with which they can hold on to trees, and good eyesight which enables them to see accurately the distances they may have to jump from branch to branch. In some cases this ability is made easier by a flap of skin between the fore and hind legs—these are the flying squirrels. Some members of the group have taken to living in the ground, using their claws to excavate extensive tunnels.

The marmots of the Old World and the prairie dogs of the New World are ground-living squirrels. The beaver is a relative of the squirrel, although it is a swimmer and cuts trees down with its sharp teeth, rather than climbing them. The twigs and bark are used for food and the heavy wood is built into a dam, with which beavers block streams. In the dam, which is made of wood and stones and mud, the beavers build their lodge—a secure house and larder, protected by the water.

The second group of rodents includes mice, voles and hamsters. The majority of these animals do man no harm. Some, like the tiny harvest mouse, are rare, due to changes in farming methods. Others, such as the golden hamster, are scarcely known in the wild, although they are familiar pets. A few, which are particularly adaptable, have become major pests. The chief of these is the brown rat, which costs mankind a great deal of money every year through damage to property, destruction of food and spread of diseases. The house mouse, although smaller, is also a pest, yet both of these species are often used in laboratory experiments which may help man. White and fancy coloured varieties of both are sometimes kept as pets.

The porcupine, the capybara, the guinea pig, the coypu and a number of South American rodents belong to the third sub-group. Protected by their spines the porcupines have few enemies other than man. The capybara and the coypu take refuge in the water, and the guinea pigs are shy animals living in dense cover, although they may become tame in captivity.

Rabbits and Hares

These familiar creatures are also gnawing animals, but they are not rodents, and are not closely related to them. They have four teeth in the upper jaw, rather than two, and these are covered with equally thick enamel all over. As a result, they cannot gnaw as well as rodents can, which is probably why there are few sorts of them. Hare-like animals are usually creatures of open country. They have long hind legs and are able to run fast over long distances to escape their enemies. Usually they are solitary, but in springtime, which is the main mating period, the jack hares become the proverbial mad March hares, leaping and cavorting about. The leverets are born in the open, for the temperate country hares do not burrow. They are fully furred at birth with their eyes open and are taken by their mothers to different hiding places.

Rabbit

Rabbits are generally smaller animals, usually living where the country has denser vegetation. The European rabbit normally burrows below ground for protection, quite large numbers of animals inhabiting the same warren. The young are born blind and helpless and remain below ground for three weeks before they emerge.

Hare

The giant anteater lives in forests in South and Central America. It moves about at night and is rarely seen by man. It feeds on ants and termites.

Toothless Mammals

Insects are generally food for small animals only, but among the mammals three groups, which include some quite large creatures, have evolved as specialised insect-eaters. These are the aardvark of Africa, the pangolins of the tropical Old World and the edentates of South and Central America. All of these animals are toothless or nearly so, and they feed chiefly on termites and ants.

The aardvark is a pig-sized creature with huge claws on its feet with which it can tear open termite heaps. It laps up the exposed insects with its 450-millimetre (eighteen-inch) long tongue. It shelters in burrows which it digs; these may be large enough for a man to creep into and are often a danger to horses or vehicles on the plains.

The pangolins look like animated fir cones, protected as they are by overlapping horny scales. Some small species live in the trees, but the giant pangolin, which is one and a half metres (five feet) long, lives entirely on the ground. They have a different digestive system from the aardvark and can deal with hard-bodied ants as well as the soft-bodied termites. Like the aardvark, they have large claws and a long tongue on which the insects are quickly caught.

In South America the edentates include the sloths, which are tree dwellers feeding on soft leaves and flowers, the armadillos, which are burrowers searching for insects and feeding also to some extent on dead flesh, and the anteaters.

The giant anteater is a forest animal, armed with such enormous claws on its front limbs that it has to walk on the sides of its feet. These claws are, however, ideal for breaking open ant and termite nests and the insects are then caught on the long sticky tongue. The giant anteater is curiously coloured with contrasting bands of black and white on its grey body. These markings help to disguise it, especially at rest, when it curls up, draping the large shaggy tail over the body. All of the toothless animals are inoffensive creatures but they are declining in numbers everywhere.

The Chinese pangolin, or scaly anteater, has a long body covered with overlapping scales

Protection

Animals are protected against their enemies in many ways. They may be able to run fast, they may have effective camouflage or they may, in some cases, carry protective weapons of armour. Among the mammals, armour is found only in the toothless insect-eating species. It consists of either bone or horn, formed in the skin and making a hard outer covering. Some, like the pangolins and the three-banded armadillo from South America (on the left) can roll up into a tight ball when frightened and so present an enemy with a tough exterior which must be dealt with before an effective attack may be made. Armadillos which have a covering of bony plates cannot in most cases roll up, but defend themselves against attack by burrowing rapidly into the earth.

The little bats are able to fly in the dark, catching their insect prey and avoiding obstacles with their sonar system.

'Seeing in the dark'
The bat's sonar is based on ultrasonic squeaks, above the level of human hearing and ranging up to 100,000 cycles per second. Each squeak lasts about one five-hundredth of a second and in normal flight the bat produces about fifty per second. Any obstruction, whether moving or stationary, causes a reflection of sound as an echo which is detected by the bat's delicate ears. The time lag between the emission of the squeak and the reception of the echo informs the animal of the distance of the obstacle. It has been shown that bats approaching an obstacle increase their rate of squeak. They can detect tiny objects in their path such as the small insects which are their prey.

Spear-nosed bat (far left). False vampire bat (left). Long-tongued fruit bat (right).

The faces of insect-eating bats (above left) appear both evil and comic, but the shape of the mouth, nose and ears is important to the animal in the way it transmits and receives the sonar signals which help it to find its way about in the dark.

Flying Mammals

Mammals are usually thought of as ground-living creatures, but nearly a quarter of all known mammal species are bats, and are capable of true flight. In developing this way of life they do not come into conflict with the birds, which fly mainly by day, for bats are strictly night-flying creatures.

How Bats Fly

The modifications of the body for flight are quite different from those found in birds. This can be seen in the skeleton which is very lightly built, but strong, especially in the region of the shoulders and chest. The wings are supported by the forelimbs and strengthened by the very much elongated finger bones which run through them. The thumb is free and may be used by the bat to manipulate food and when moving about the walls of its roost. The wing membrane, which is made of soft skin and involves no feathers, is stretched from the shoulder to the ankle and sometimes continues to include the tail.

Bat's legs are swivelled at the hip joint so that the knee bends in the opposite direction from that of other mammals, but this helps to tension the trailing edge of the wing. Flight varies from the erratic fluttering of some of the tiny bats to the sustained flight of the larger species, some of which are capable of long migrations. Flight requires the output of a great deal of energy, and bats save this energy by becoming more or less inactive when they are not flying.

Bats are classified into two great groups, the big bats, which are all found in the tropical Old World and are fruit-eaters, and the little bats, found throughout the world. The little bats are flesh-eaters, most species feeding on night-flying insects, but some feed on fish or, in the case of vampires, on blood. Most bats are entirely harmless to man and the fear which they inspire is probably caused by their dark colour, their silent night flight and their curious faces.

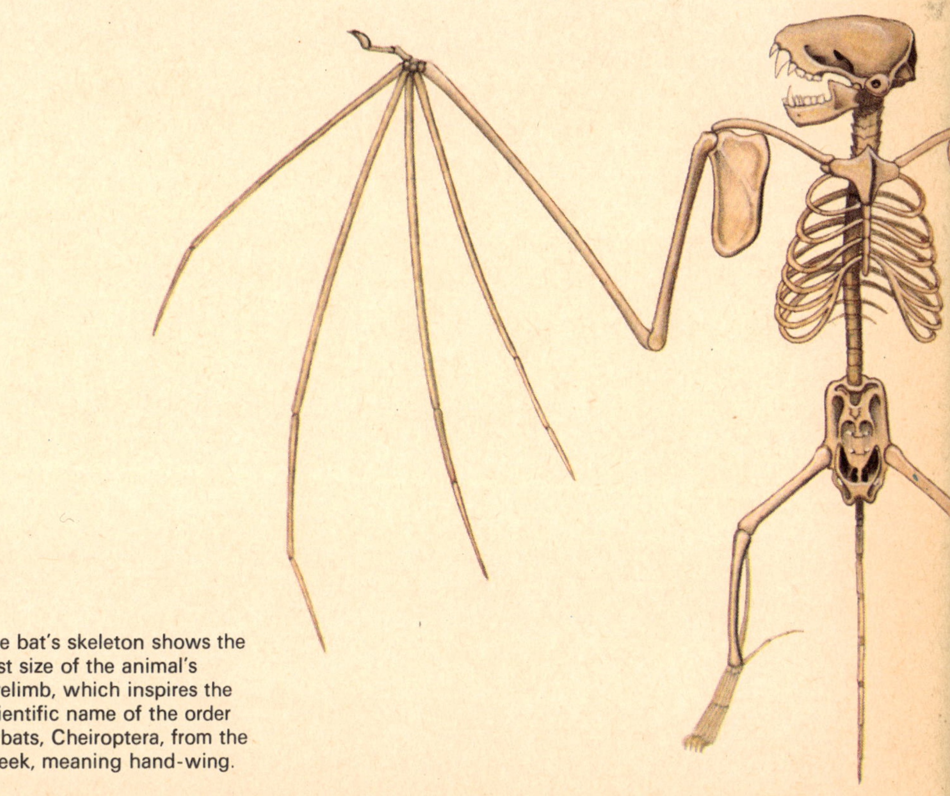

The bat's skeleton shows the vast size of the animal's forelimb, which inspires the scientific name of the order of bats, Cheiroptera, from the Greek, meaning hand-wing.

Bottle-nosed dolphins

Marine Mammals

With a group of animals as successful as the mammals, it is not surprising that some of them should have taken to the sea for their way of life. Three separate orders, the whales, the sea cows and the seals, are now totally aquatic and so highly adapted for this life that most cannot survive on land. In the case of the seals, they never depart far from the water where they are most at home.

Underwater sounds
Whales are mostly sociable animals and schools of them may be heard conversing with clicking and squeaking noises quite audible to human ears. They also make sounds far above the level of human hearing, emitted as high-pitched bursts of sound, coming from the blowhole. These are used for echo-location of prey and obstacles in the water. Although there is no external ear, whales have exceedingly acute hearing and can detect subtle differences in the quality of the echoes.

Demands of the Sea

The sea makes many demands on its inhabitants and mammals adapted to live in it demonstrate these in their structure. Compared with air, water is very dense and successful locomotion demands that the animal should be streamlined. All marine mammals are sleek, curved creatures, presenting little obstacle to the smooth flow of water over their bodies. The sea is cold, so all marine mammals are protected by a thick deposit of fat under the skin. It is also a protection against many enemies and a support to weight, so most marine mammals are large and heavily built.

However well adapted to the sea marine mammals appear to be, they have all descended from land-living ancestors and they retain many features characteristic of land animals. The skeleton of the flipper of a whale, for instance, is exactly comparable to a human arm and hand and very different in structure from the fin of a fish. All marine mammals produce living young and suckle them, showing parental care typical of their land-living relatives. Also, marine mammals have to come to the surface to breathe. Although they can hold their breath much longer than land mammals, their lungs are similar and they cannot extract oxygen from the water as fishes can.

The whales are the most completely aquatic of the mammals. Although a few inhabit rivers, most are creatures of the open oceans. They are perfectly designed for life in the water, swimming by means of a horizontal tail fluke, or lobe. Their hind legs are reduced to a small remnant of internal bone and their forelimbs modified to form balancing flippers. They have no external ears and no fur to diminish their streamlining—the only hair present on their bodies being a small moustache found in some species.

There are two great groups of whales: the toothed whales and the baleen whales. The first group contains all of the small species and a few large ones, such as the sperm whale. They usually have a large number of pointed teeth, suitable for catching the fishes and squids which are their food. In some cases the teeth have become reduced in number, as for example in the narwhal, in which the female has no teeth at all and the male has only one tooth, a long, twisted incisor growing straight forward out of the mouth.

Baleen Whales

The baleen whales are all large. They include the blue whale, which may be over thirty metres (100 feet) long and weigh more than 120 tons. It is the biggest animal ever to have lived on earth. All baleen whales are toothless, but they have instead a series of triangular plates of material, a substance like fingernails, hanging from the roof of the mouth. These are the baleen plates, which on their inner edges are broken into a fine, hair-like fringe, although they are quite smooth on the outer, cheek side.

Baleen whales spend much of their lives in sub-polar regions where the rich nutrients in the water allow the growth of many marine plants and small animals. These in turn nourish shrimp-like creatures called krill which are the food of the largest whales. The baleen whale swims slowly through the huge schools of krill, taking water containing the shrimps

The male narwhal has an enormous spirally twisted tusk, probably used in mating fights.

into its immense mouth. The water is expelled, usually by a rolling movement, but the krill get trapped in the fringed baleen and from here they are swallowed.

Some whales are said to be able to hold their breath for over two hours. Although their brains, which are large and active, must have oxygen, their bodies can run short for a while. This is called building up an oxygen debt, but this must be repaid when the animal comes up to breathe and it accounts for the fact that many whales pant noisily when breathing. When they are living in polar seas the air above the water is cold and causes condensation of the water vapour in their breath. This is the major part of the characteristic spout, or blow, of the whale. In toothed whales it forms a single cloud; in the baleen species a double spout, formed from the two separate nostrils of the blowhole, or nose. Whales also often blow out a fatty material which lines the air passages, and this may be seen as a thin cloud, even in warm-water areas. They do not blow out fountains of water. A whale with water in its lungs would drown, as surely as would any other mammal.

At the top of the page are sperm whales seen coming to the surface to 'blow'. The mighty blue whale is the greatest animal ever to have lived. In comparison, it dwarfs the largest modern mammal, the elephant.

Mermaid legends
Legends of sea maidens, singing enchanting songs, combing their golden tresses or cradling their young in their arms, are widespread. The source of these stories is to be found in the sea cows, a group of aquatic mammals of tropical waters, quite unrelated to land cows. Few animals could be less like the romantic image of the mermaid, for these heavyweight, placid creatures have a fish-like form with expanded tail flukes, forelimbs transformed into flippers and hairless bodies, although the face has heavy bristles. The young have a fairly long suckling period and while being fed are supported in their mother's flippers. A short-sighted sailor might, in a poor light, suppose that one of these creatures was akin to the women that he had not seen for a long while, but a closer look would bring disillusion. In order to feed, sea cows must be near to land, for their diet consists of coastal seaweeds.

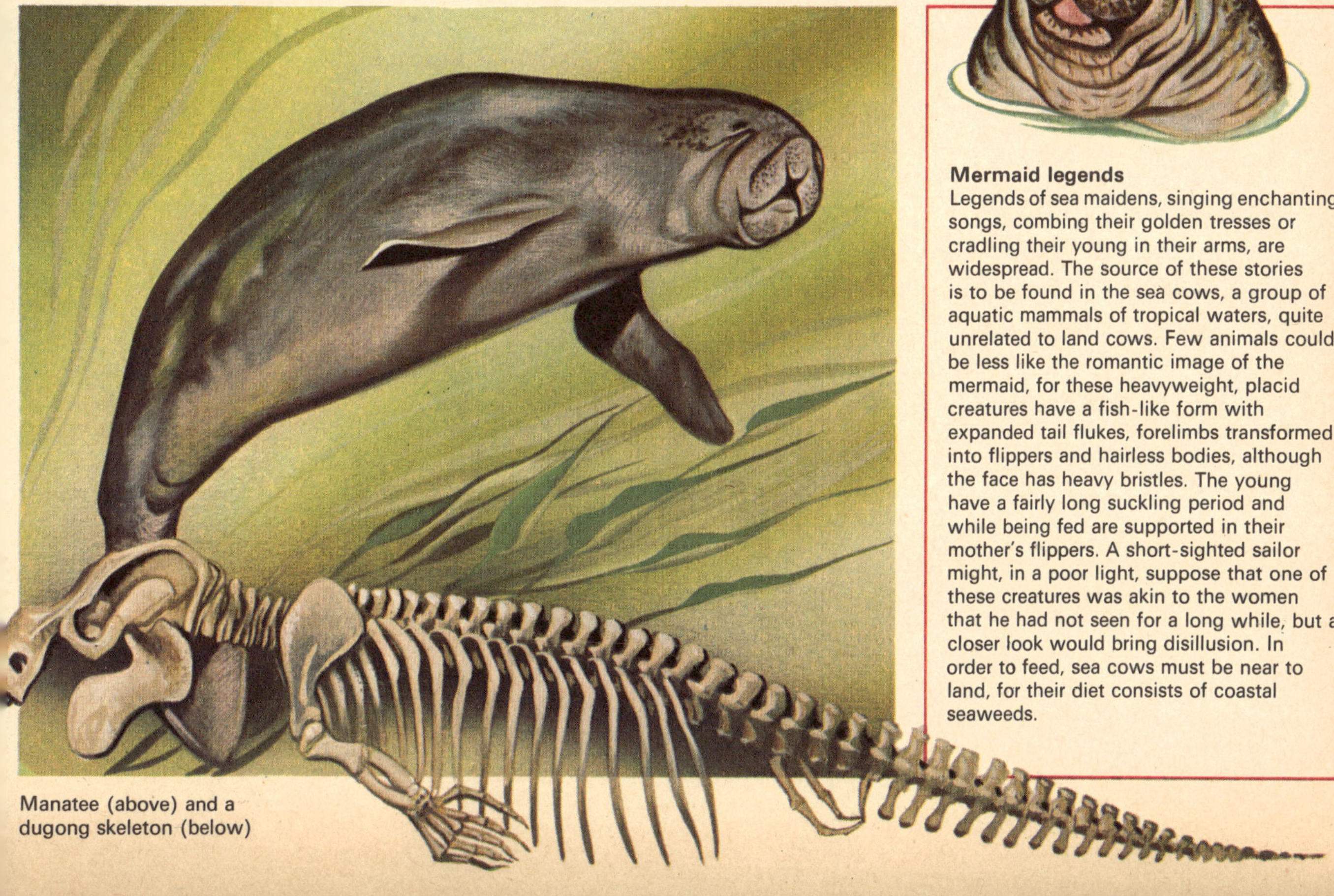

Manatee (above) and a dugong skeleton (below)

Elephant seal

Seals

Seals are the third order of aquatic mammals. They are sometimes thought to be closely related to land carnivores but modern research shows that they have a separate ancestry, so they are placed in a special order, called the Pinnepedia.

In seals all four limbs are present, but they are transformed into paddles. In the true seals the hind limbs are twisted backwards and are used in a side-to-side motion in swimming. This is like the action of a fish's tail and the animals swim in a graceful, sinuous way. On land, however, they are helpless and have to hitch themselves along, using their front flippers and a humping, caterpillar-like movement of the body.

The other two groups, the eared seals and the walrus, swim using their large fore-flippers and steer with the hind. They can turn their hind feet under the body and can move on land with a clumsy, galloping gait. All seals have dense hair covering their bodies. In some species this is especially fine and rich and forms a heavy cape over the shoulders. As well as fur, seals have a heavy layer of blubber underneath the skin, which in the case of the elephant seal may be several inches thick.

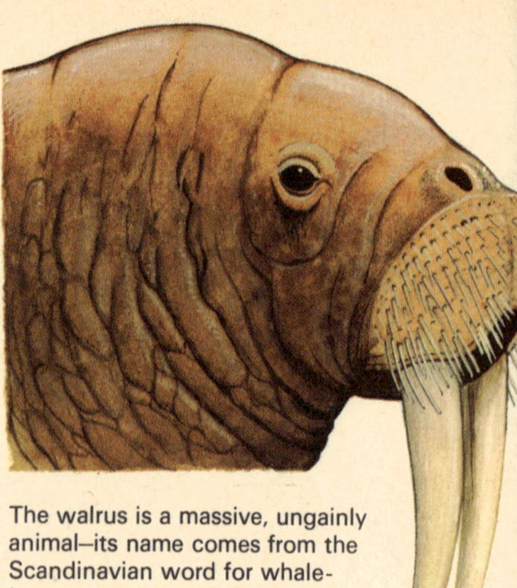

The walrus is a massive, ungainly animal–its name comes from the Scandinavian word for whale-horse–and the adult animal has a pair of very long tusks which it uses in fighting and to haul itself along and clamber out of water.

Seals are divided into two families, the true or earless seals (below) and the eared seals. The latter, such as the fur seal above, have obvious external ears and hind limbs.

The crab-eating seal (above) is the common seal of Antarctic waters. Its coat fades during the year to become a creamy white.

The dark grey, ringed seal lives in the extreme north, mostly in Arctic waters.

In spite of their adaptations to water, the seals have to return to land to reproduce. In some polar species they do this on ice floes, but generally they congregate in rookeries on remote rocky shores and islands. The males come ashore first to stake out their breeding territories. There is often a great deal of fighting, which looks and sounds terrifying, the bulls rearing up and roaring, sparring and slashing with their large canine teeth. Injuries are often severe, but fatalities are rare. The male elephant seal, which weighs over two tons, is made more fearsome by his huge inflated snout, which acts as a sounding box for his roars.

In some cases females are allowed to pass into the territory of any male they choose. In others, the females are herded into the harems of the biggest males and not allowed to leave. When the pups are born the mothers are permitted to return to the sea to feed, for they must keep up their reserves so they can provide their young with plenty of fat-rich milk. Soon after this they mate again and although in some cases they stay ashore, feeding their cubs for nearly three months, in others they return to the sea in about three weeks.

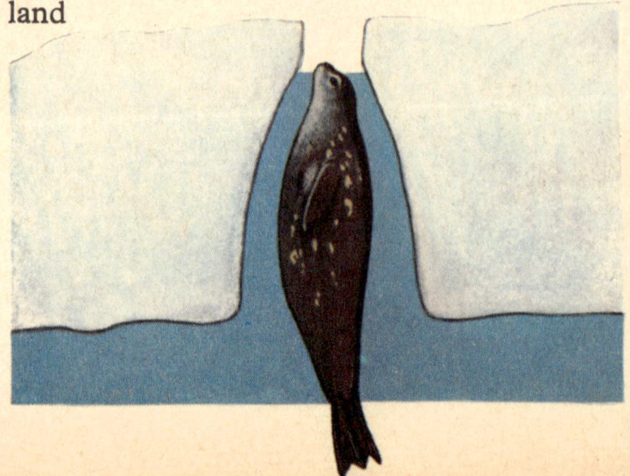

In Arctic regions seals remain in the area of pack and shelf ice, but since they have to breathe air they keep open holes in the ice. In the Antarctic, Weddell's seal gnaws through the ice as it forms. It is probable that tooth wear eventually prevents some of these seals from keeping their breathing holes open, so many of the older animals drown.

Hoofed Mammals

In some plant-eating animals which have no defence from their enemies but their speed and endurance when they run away, the toenails have developed into sheathing hooves. These protect the feet and enable them to travel without damage for long distances over hard ground. Two great groups of hoofed animals exist, those with an odd number of toes and those which have two or four toes to each of their feet. The odd-toed hoofed mammals include all of the horse-like animals, the tapirs and the rhinoceroses.

Wild Horses

The horse-like species are creatures of the plains. They live in herds and are extremely wary, their keen senses of smell and hearing and magnificent eyesight informing them of any danger. Each leg narrows to a single hard hoof and every step that they take is of maximum length, for they are, in effect, running on the tips of their toes. A single young one is born at a time and is capable of keeping up with the herd shortly after birth. Grass is their chief food and to combat the wear of such a harsh diet, the teeth are open-rooted and go on growing throughout the animals' lives.

The true wild horses of eastern Asia are now extremely rare, although in late prehistoric times they were probably the commonest open-country creatures from western Europe across the plains of Asia. It is from these animals that the domestic breeds of horse have been derived. The 'half asses' of western Asia and the true asses of North Africa are also nearly extinct. The zebras of Africa are the only abundant surviving members of the group. These are adapted to tropical grasslands, where they may still be seen in some numbers.

Tapirs are forest-living animals, which have three toes on their hind feet, but four, including one very small one, on the front feet. They are found in Malaya and in central and tropical South America. They are shy, solitary animals, taking refuge in water if they are chased by any enemies.

Rhinoceroses

The rhinoceroses are the heavyweight members of the group. In distant prehistoric times there were many kinds of rhinoceros; now there are only five, of which three are in serious danger of extinction. All are large, grey, heavy-skinned animals, distinguished by one or sometimes

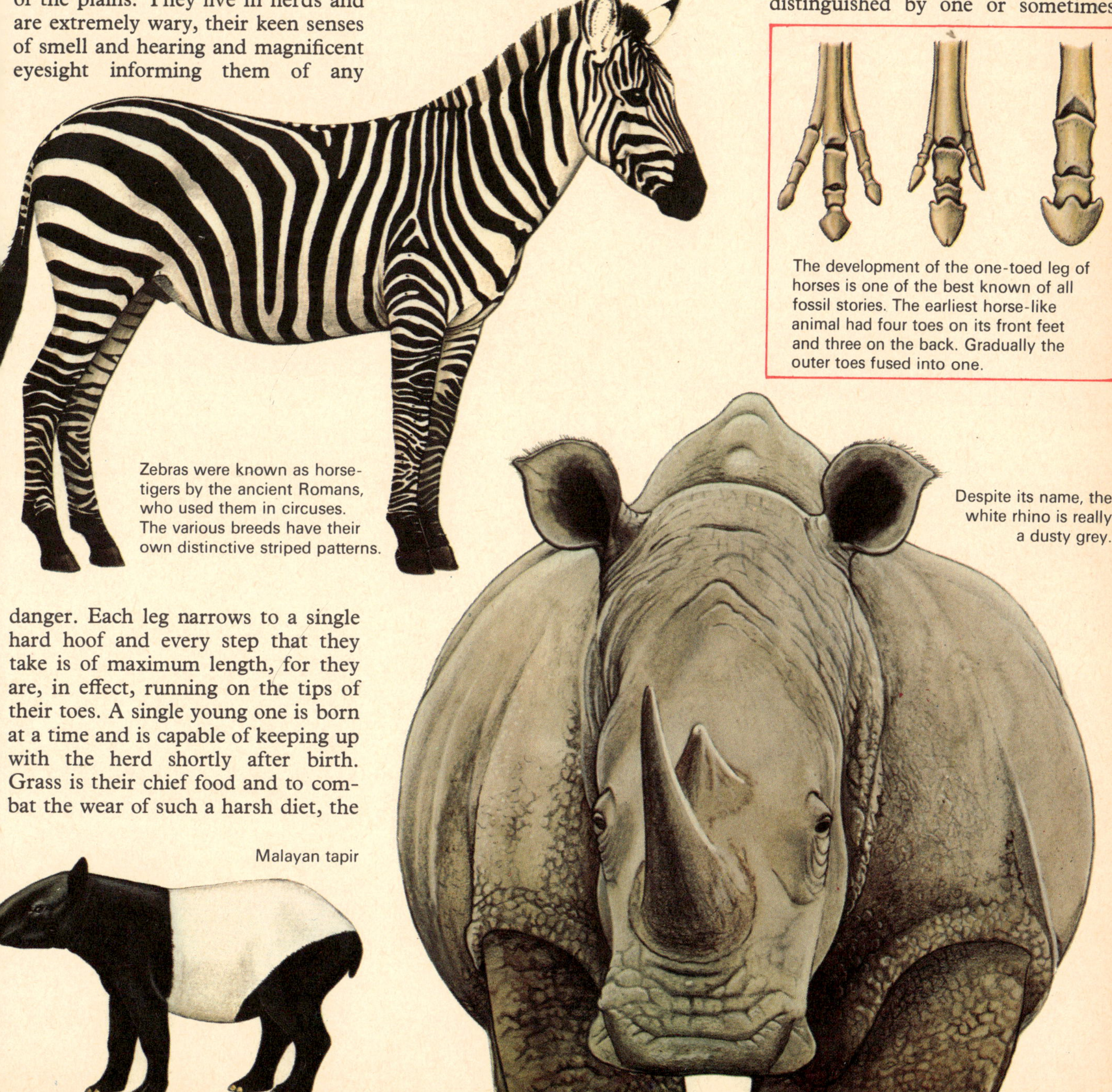

The development of the one-toed leg of horses is one of the best known of all fossil stories. The earliest horse-like animal had four toes on its front feet and three on the back. Gradually the outer toes fused into one.

Zebras were known as horse-tigers by the ancient Romans, who used them in circuses. The various breeds have their own distinctive striped patterns.

Despite its name, the white rhino is really a dusty grey.

Malayan tapir

two horns on the end of the nose. These are not true horn but are made of compressed hair. Most rhinoceroses are forest or bush animals, with pointed upper lips which aid them in browsing leaves from trees. The African white rhino (white being a corruption of the Afrikaans word for wide and having no reference to the colour of the animal) is a grazer and feeds on grasses in fairly open country.

The even-toed hoofed animals are a much more flourishing group than the odd-toed, and the vast majority of medium to large-sized, plant-eating mammals belong to it. Although many of them are now rare few are so close to extinction as the wild horses or the rhinos.

Even-toed animals have also gone up on to the tips of their toes but the weight is borne by the third and fourth toe of each foot. Each toe carries a large nail, giving the typical cloven-hoofed appearance of the group. In many cases the fifth and second toes are also present, but they rarely take any of the animal's weight. The difference in weight-bearing toes is reflected in completely different systems of balance in the two groups of hoofed animals. This shows in many features of their life; an easy one to observe is the way in which the animals rise from a lying position. A horse gets up fore feet first; a cow hind feet first. When they graze, many even-toed animals stoop down to the herbage, putting their weight on the 'wrists' of their front legs, something never seen in the odd-toed.

When it drinks, the giraffe must spread its legs wide apart so that its head can reach the water.

Pigs and Hippos

Pigs are the least specialised members of the order. They are medium-sized animals found throughout the forested regions of the world except Australasia. Hippos, which now survive only in Africa, are also structurally primitive but highly adapted to life in lakes or slow-flowing rivers.

Camels

Camels, which are found in Africa and Asia, are closely related to the llamas and vicuñas of South America. These are all animals of arid areas with two toes on their tough, padded feet, and thick protective fur which insulates them against great heat and the cold of desert nights. The camel has the ability to survive long periods without food or water. This led to their being of great value as a means of transport in desert regions. In Africa the one-humped camel, or dromedary, is found. This animal is totally domesticated and no wild ancestors are known. In Asia the two-humped Bactrian camel occurs. Recently, wild relatives of this domestic species have been found, but they are extremely rare.

The okapi is a rare Congo animal, discovered by Europeans in 1900.

When nothing else is available camels can feed on dry thorn scrub, digesting what they eat very completely by means of their complex three-chambered stomach. When water is scarce, they are capable of much greater endurance without it than any other mammals, but when it becomes available again they make up the lack very rapidly. A camel may drink more than 130 litres (thirty gallons) at one time under such circumstances.

All the rest of the even-toed animals share a number of characteristics not found in pigs, hippos or camels. The most obvious is the development on the heads of most of the males and some females, of bony outgrowths—antlers in deer and horns in sheep, cattle and antelopes. They all have a more complex digestive system, gathering their food very rapidly and then retiring to some safe spot for digestion. During this, they return the food to the mouth from the first, or storage, compartment of a four-chambered stomach to chew the cud.

Deer

The deer are the major even-toed group of the temperate world. Although there are some tropical species the majority are animals of deciduous and coniferous woodlands and the most northerly species, the reindeer (caribou of North America), migrates into the tundra for the summer months. They are mostly herd animals, with, in some cases, shifting groups of males and females at different times of the year.

The antlers of deer, present in the males only, except in the reindeer where the females have small growths,

The camel's upper lip overhangs the lower and its slit-like nostrils can be closed at will. Its two-toed foot has pads which spread its weight on loose sand.

The Bactrian camel has a double hump. With its shorter legs and bulkier build it is better suited to the rocky, hilly country of Central Asia than to the sandy deserts of Arabia.

are bony outgrowths from permanent knobs on the skull, called the pedicles. In the young deer the antlers are small and simple but they are shed and regrown annually, and as the animal ages they become bigger and more complex. This is a considerable strain on the system. Deer which are poorly fed usually grow small antlers, and among red deer an abnormal male without antlers is usually a bigger and heavier beast than the stags which have them.

It is likely that antlers evolved as a device for spreading scent during the mating season, or rut. Now this has become a secondary purpose and the main use is in the battles waged by the males for mates. Fighting stags lock antlers and push at each other. When one feels that he can no longer compete, a sideways movement allows him to disengage and run away. In spite of the noise of deer battles, fatalities are rare, for the winner remains with the harem for which he has been fighting and the loser will not return.

Giraffes

Giraffes are tropical relatives of the deer. On their curiously shaped heads are bony outgrowths which are in effect pedicles, very occasionally carrying small antlers. Some prehistoric giraffes had huge antlers, but these creatures are now quite extinct. When they fight, giraffes swing their heads against each other. The force of the blows must be considerable, for the bone is heavy and thickens during the animal's life; an old male giraffe may have a head weighing eleven kilograms (twenty-four pounds), but in spite of this, little damage seems to be done. Their long legs and necks, which have the same number of joints as other mammals, enable them to reach the upper foliage of the trees of the savannah country where they live. Their tongues are also extraordinarily long and can pluck tiny leaves from among the thorns carried by many trees.

Drinking is for a giraffe a most difficult matter. It must either spread its legs or bend its wrist joints so that its head may reach the water. There are other problems too in having such a long neck, one of them being the control of blood to and from the brain. Giraffes have special valves in the blood vessels of their necks to keep the flow steady whether the head is up or down. Many variations on the colour camouflage patterns of the giraffe have been described, but there is only one species found (in suitable areas) throughout most of Africa.

The distinctive feature of the deer family is the branched growth on the skull called antlers, but not all deer possess them. Antlers grow from bony knobs in the skull and are shed each year when they are developed to their fullest extent.

Arabian camel, or dromedary

The cattle, sheep, goats and antelopes are all horned animals. They are found in suitable country throughout the world, except Australia, and have colonised many types of habitat, including plains, swamps, forests and mountains. They usually produce only one young at a time, and it is active soon after birth. All northern domestic cattle are descended from the aurochs, an animal common in Europe in prehistoric times, but extinct since the seventeenth century.

The water buffalo is another cow-like horned animal widely domesticated in the Far East, but the cape buffalo of Africa is one of the most feared of game animals. It is said to be aggressive and dangerous, especially if frightened or wounded. The yak is a mountain animal of Central Asia, capable of surviving in barren uplands but not able to thrive in lush lowland areas. In domestication it may be crossed with cattle, but the pure form is used for milk, meat, hides and transport in the upper heights of the Himalayas.

Sheep and Goats

Sheep and goats are also animals of arid upland areas. The sheep, which have huge curved horns, are hairy and do not have the thick fleeces of advanced domestic breeds. They are sure-footed creatures capable of taking to the highest slopes when danger threatens. The bighorn sheep of North America, which is the only sheep in the New World, is found at high levels in the northern Rockies.

Goats have horns which may be very large, but they are scimitar shaped and do not spiral. In some of the species of ibex they may measure more than one and a half metres (five feet) long. They have been prized trophies for hunters, a fact which has contributed to their decline throughout their range. They are stocky looking animals, yet they have incredible agility and can find footholds on almost sheer rock faces.

Antelopes have evolved a great variety of horns. The species seen here are (left to right) gnu, nilgai, kudu, sable antelope, oryx, hartebeeste and eland.

In Europe, man's long occupation of the steppes has removed all large wild animals, but when white men first went to North America they found one large mammal dominant on the prairies. This was the American bison, often called the buffalo. It is estimated that the herds of bison numbered over 60 million animals in the days before the white man. Moving over the prairies, they were central to the fertility of the plains and the key figure in the economy of plants, other animals and man, for the Plains Indians had developed a way of life totally dependent on them. Partly in order to clear the land for agriculture and partly to subdue the Indians, a great campaign of destruction of the bison went on during the nineteenth century. Whole herds were destroyed; in many cases the carcasses and skins remained unused.

Antelopes

The antelopes are the largest and most varied group of the even-toed mammals. They are all found in the Old World, chiefly in Africa where they range in size from the tiny pygmy antelopes of dense scrubland in East Africa to the eland, which stands up to 1·8 metres (six feet) at the shoulder. Almost all are good runners and some can make spectacular leaps as well. This is one of the features which has made them difficult to domesticate, for they are capable of jumping out of almost any enclosure. Most of the antelopes are herd animals, sometimes congregating in vast numbers, especially when on migration. Although they have been much reduced in recent years, some species are still widespread and numerous. The horns of antelopes are extremely varied in shape, ranging from the tiny straight points of the dik-diks to the knurled scimitars of the giant sable antelope, which may measure well over one and a half metres (five feet) in length. In some cases, such as the kudu, they form an open, corkscrew-like spiral, in others the curve is lyre-shaped while the oryx species generally have long straight horns.

In the past, antelopes were regarded as game animals to be hunted, or destroyed and replaced with domestic species if the land was to be farmed. Now in many places attempts are being made to tame them for the milk and meat which they could give. They are immune to many of the diseases which can kill off introduced farm animals and some species may be the future domestic animals of the tropics. An Asiatic antelope, the saiga, has, by careful conservation, been brought from the brink of extinction to large numbers again, and controlled cropping is now practised.

Elephants

Elephants are the largest land animals of the present day. Living in herds in the tropics of Africa and Asia, they are the remnants of a worldwide group which at one time colonised every continent except Australia and Antarctica, and occupied all types of environment including the tundra. Elephants are unmistakable; apart from their large size no other animal has tusks or trunk as they do. Its trunk is the elephant's lifeline. Through it he breathes and tests the air for alien scents; with it he collects food, ranging from berries which can be plucked individually with the sensitive finger-like tip, to whole trees which may be broken down. The trunk is used for drinking and for picking up dry earth with which the elephant dusts its body, probably as a protection against flies. The tusks are open-rooted incisor teeth which grow throughout the life of the animal; they tend to be larger in males than in females. The largest recorded was over $3\frac{1}{2}$ metres (twelve feet) in length and weighed over 90 kilograms (200 pounds). They are used as levers when trees are to be broken or uprooted for food; for boring for water, or digging up earth which will be eaten because it contains necessary minerals, and in defence.

Plant-eaters

Elephants are herbivores, eating a wide range of plants. They grind their food with large teeth placed far back in the mouth. These eventually wear out, but others grow in their place. In the course of an elephant's life it has twenty-six teeth—two tusks and twenty-four grinding teeth. For all of its life an elephant is, in effect, teething and when its last molars wear out the animal can no longer feed efficiently, so its lifespan is to a large extent determined by its teeth. Elephants need to eat a great deal and spend much of every day feeding. They may travel long distances looking for food and water, which they must also have in large quantities. Although an adult elephant has no enemies other than man, lions or tigers might attack the young and elephants are always alert to this possibility, their senses of hearing and smell in particular warning them of any danger.

The principal differences between the African elephant (above) and the Asiatic, or Indian, elephant (below) are the greater bulk and bigger ears of the African species and the high, domed forehead of the Asiatic.

Family group of African elephants

Carnivores

The carnivores form an extremely varied group of animals, unified by their adaptations for feeding on flesh. They range in size from tiny weasels to giant bears; the pattern of their coats may be spotted, striped or in plain colours; they may have long tails or no tails, but the fact that they are hunters gives them a number of features in common. Many of these can be seen in the skull, which always has a fairly large brain case, for carnivores are intelligent animals and must be able to outwit their prey. The eyes are large and usually point well forwards, which gives them a fair degree of three-dimensional vision, necessary for pouncing on and catching prey.

In most carnivores there are six small nipping teeth across the front of the jaw. These are followed by the canine teeth, which are long and pointed. They are used for slashing and in some cases for gripping so that the teeth in the back of the mouth can work to better advantage. Behind the canines, the pre-molar and molar teeth are generally narrow and give a cutting edge. In most carnivores one cheek tooth is greatly enlarged for slicing action. The jaw-hinge of carnivores is a very tight one, allowing no sideways movement as in ourselves or in most of the plant eaters: instead the jaws work like scissors and the typical meat eater cuts its food into pieces just small enough to swallow, and bolts it down.

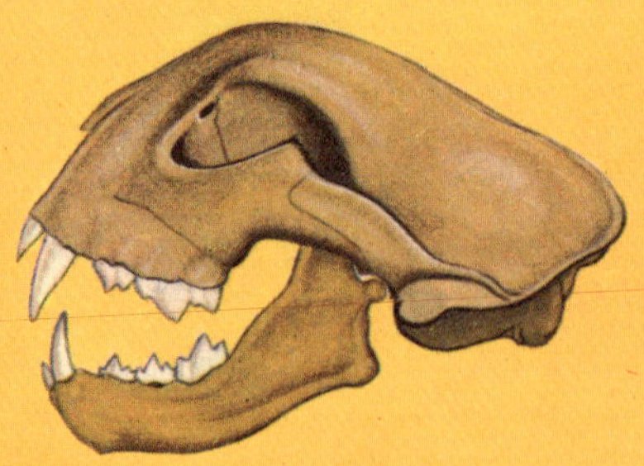

Over short distances the cheetah (top) can probably run faster than any other mammal. The snarling tiger (right) reveals the enlarged canine teeth typical of carnivores, seen also in the skull above.

Male lion

The carnivores may be classified into two main groups of animals: those related to the dogs and those nearer to the cats. The dogs, bears, pandas and weasels are related, while the cats, hyenas and civets form the other group. Each of these groups has, over a long period of time, followed particular lines of development.

The Cat Group

The cat group, which contains the 'big cats' such as tigers, lions and leopards, also includes many small creatures such as the ocelot, the Scottish wildcat and the domestic cat, which is probably of Egyptian origin. Cats all hunt their prey by stalking, followed by a brief sprint. The bored domestic cat hunting sparrows and the lion or cheetah after antelopes use the same technique.

The cheetah, which is said to be the speediest of all mammals, is reputed to touch 110 kilometres (70 miles) per hour, but it never keeps up this speed for long. If it cannot catch its prey within a sprint of 180 metres (200 yards) it gives up and later tries to stalk closer before giving its presence away with a speedy dash. For this type of hunting, cats need, and have, good eyesight and excellent hearing, but their sense of smell is not so good as that of the dogs.

Members of the cat family often kill using their feet, which are armed with large, usually retractile claws. They are mostly solitary animals, but an exception is to be found in the lion, which is social, living in groups or prides of up to twenty animals. Lions, or more usually lionesses, may hunt communally and so are able to bring down larger and more dangerous prey than could be killed by a single animal. Lions are now found only in Africa and a very few in India. In the historic past the areas of the Middle East which are now mainly desert were sufficiently fertile to support many animals and the lions that preyed on them, but these conditions no longer exist.

Common otter

The Weasel Family
Central to the weasel family, which is found mainly in the northern temperate parts of the world, are the weasels themselves and stoats. They are small animals with long bodies and short legs and an undulating way of moving. The female weasel is a tiny creature. Both she and her mate are able to enter mouseholes to catch their main food. Stoats are slightly larger and hunt bigger prey, especially rabbits. Often a stoat will mesmerise a rabbit by leaping and gambolling, but will come closer until it is near enough to catch it. Both stoats and weasels sometimes keep their young with them until they are nearly adult, and this gives rise to stories of packs of these animals hunting together.

Hyenas

Hyenas are scavengers, living on the plains of Africa. They have powerful jaws with teeth strong enough to crack the leg bones of antelopes, which is often all that a lion will leave of its kill. If there are no pickings from the remains of meals of the bigger predators, hyenas will hunt for themselves, often catching zebra. The civets and their relatives are short-legged hunters of the tropics. They feed on a wide variety of food, including in many instances snakes and rodents, so they are often welcome in the region of homesteads.

The Dog Family

The members of the dog family, which includes wolves, jackals, coyotes and foxes, are all long-distance runners, tiring their prey and pulling it down after a chase which may have covered several miles. All of the dogs are medium to small-sized animals; even a large wolf may be only one quarter the weight of a lion. They all tend to have long legs, a good sense of hearing and a very good sense of smell, which they may need to use when hunting.

With the exception of foxes, dogs are highly social animals, with a family and pack structure of considerable complexity. The domestic dog, which is almost certainly descended from wolf ancestors, shows this to some extent, but in most cases grown-up dogs have behaviour patterns more suited to wolf cubs than to adult animals. This can be seen in many features, but an obvious one is the noisiness of dogs compared to wolves. Wolf cubs yap, but the adults, apart from the howling parties which sometimes precede a hunt, are relatively silent animals. Domestic dogs tend to be noisy at all times, a feature which could easily lead to disaster for a wild animal.

All carnivores, whether solitary or social, have a prolonged childhood. During this period they may be reared solely by their mother, as with bears or tigers; by both parents, as with foxes; or as members of a pack in which aunts and uncles play a large part in their upbringing, as with wolves. During this time they are taught the main things that they should know—how to make a kill and how to defend themselves, for example. In spite of this, all carnivores

Timber wolf

eat a certain amount of plant material. In some, such as bears or badgers, it is a very high proportion of their total food; in others, such as cats or weasels, it is a small proportion only. But meat by itself is not an adequate diet and some plant food is always taken.

Bears

Most carnivores are not large animals. There is usually an abundance of plant food to keep big herbivores (plant eaters) going, but the quantities of meat required for a large flesh eater may well not be available. The only really large carnivores are the bears and these animals have taken to a more varied diet, as can be seen by their flat-topped teeth, with none of the meat-slicing ability of the other members of the order, although they will often eat flesh in preference to other things.

Bears are found chiefly in the northern hemisphere and can be considered as belonging to three main groups: the brown bears, the black bears and the polar bear. The brown bears are to be found in North America, Europe and Asia and although they may vary considerably in size they are not significantly different from each other. The black bears are more varied. They include the American black bears and a number of Asiatic species, including the sloth bear of India. The polar bear is an Arctic species, spending much of its time hunting seals on the northern pack ice, often floating far out to sea as the floes break up.

One of the rarest mammals is the giant panda which lives in China and Tibet.

Polar bear

Bears are distinguished from all other carnivores by the nature of their teeth. Their molars are adapted for grinding, and the crowns are almost flat. They are best seen in a typical bear skull, demonstrating the vegetarian nature of the bear's diet.

Brown bear

Bears feed hugely during the summer and autumn months, when they become very fat. They then den up for the winter in a warm safe place, and snooze through until next spring, but they do not truly hibernate. It is at this time that bear cubs are born. Relative to the size of their mothers, they are the smallest young of any of the placental mammals. A female grizzly, weighing over 220 kilograms (500 pounds), will give birth to cubs weighing a few ounces each. They remain with her in the den, suckling, but making relatively small demands on her until the end of the winter, by which time they are able to come out and begin to feed themselves, although they will probably remain with their mother for three years in all.

The Giant Panda

The giant panda looks bear-like, but this is because, as with the bears, it is a carnivore which has taken to a diet consisting largely of plants. It is one of the rarest of mammals, being found only in the bamboo thicket zone of high mountains in south-west China. The red panda, which is smaller, has a wider distribution through the south-eastern Himalayas. It feeds on fruit, small animals and birds' eggs. Both of these animals are related to a group of American creatures. They include the raccoon, which can climb trees but feeds in streams on fresh-water crabs or shells; the coatimundi, which is a forest animal feeding on vegetation and small animals including insects; and the kinkajou, which feeds entirely on soft fruit. This strange creature looks more like a monkey than anything else, but it is structurally a carnivore.

Red panda

Primates

This name has been given to a group of animals whose members at first sight appear to have little in common. They include some animals which are little different from the insectivores, as well as lemurs, monkeys, apes and man. Many of the features which are used to distinguish them are found also in other animals, but not in the combination in which they occur in the primates. These features include an enlarged brain case and complex brain; forward-looking eyes contained in bony orbits in the skull, hands and feet on which there are five digits, and nails rather than claws on at least some of the fingers and toes.

Tree Shrews and Lemurs

The tree shrews are the most primitive of the primates. As their name suggests, they are insectivore-like in many ways, but their brain structure is similar to that of some of the lemurs, and their hands and feet show some development towards a grasping ability, in spite of having claws rather than nails on each toe. Squirrel-like in appearance they have a degree of activity and curiosity which accords with primates rather than any other group.

The lemurs are more advanced in their primate characteristics. They are all rather small nocturnal animals, with a coat of thick fur and a long bushy tail. Their eyes point fairly well forwards, but in most cases they have a distinct snout, which means rather poor three-dimensional sight. They are found only in the Old World, especially in Madagascar where it seems that isolated populations of lemurs developed along specialised lines for a long period of time. Some of these animals are agile forest dwellers; others, such as the mouse lemurs, are small animals of drier areas.

The Aye-aye

The aye-aye is a strange creature adapted to feeding on grubs in dead wood. It has chisel-like teeth in the front of its mouth for tearing the wood open and a long thin finger for hooking out any grubs that may be there. In Africa the lemurs are represented by the bush babies and the potto and in India by the lorises. These animals are small, slender, tail-less creatures, moving through the branches of their forest home with great deliberation and slowness. They hold very firmly on to branches with hands and feet in which the index finger and second toes have become much reduced. Once they have decided to grasp anything firmly they are very difficult to dislodge.

The man-like primates include the monkeys, apes and man. There is sufficient obvious similarity between

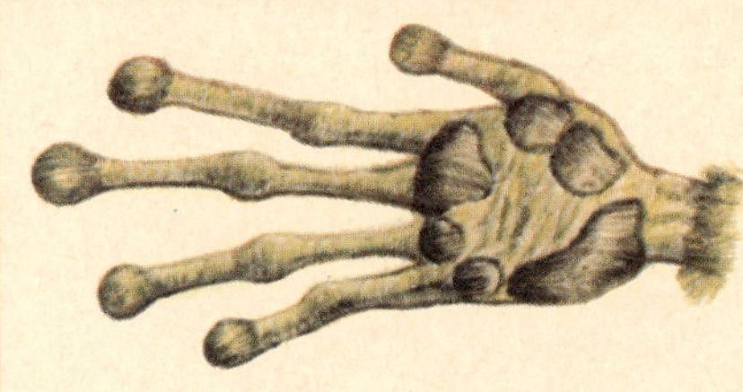

The tarsier is an animal from a once abundant group of early primates now surviving in south-east Asia. It shows the development of characteristics which in the past led to the higher members of this group. The tarsier is awake at night and very active, leaping from twig to twig in the forest, grasping and hanging on with hands and feet. The hands of the tarsier set the scene for later primate hands. All five digits are well grown, the thumb is separate from the rest of the fingers and opposable, so that objects can be grasped and held firmly and, if need be, examined. Each finger has a nail and beneath it a fleshy pad, which adds to the sensitivity of the finger tip. The skin of the pad is deeply creased and forms a friction area which enables the animal to gain a grip, even on extremely smooth surfaces.

The tarsier (above) and the slender loris (left) are primitive members of the primate group to which man himself belongs.

these three for the relationship to be clear, but man is not the descendant of any of the living species of ape or monkey. A common ancestor with the apes must be looked for among fossils which date back 30 million years; for an ancestor shared with monkeys we would have to go back nearer 50 million years.

New World Monkeys

Monkeys are essentially tree-living creatures of tropical forests. A few species, such as the baboons, spend a great deal of time on the ground and some, such as the langurs of the Himalayas and the monkeys of Japan, can survive in cold climates, but these are exceptions to the general rule. The monkeys of South America are thought to be more primitive because of such features as their dense fur and their long tails, which are never reduced in length. They have a larger number of teeth than the Old World monkeys. Many species carry claws rather than nails on at least some of their fingers and toes.

Some of the South American monkeys have prehensile tails, which means they can be used to grasp things. Monkeys support their whole weight on this extra 'limb' as they swing through the trees. Most of them are social, living in family groups and travelling through the treetops. Howler monkeys make themselves obvious by their howling concerts, in which the sound may carry for several miles through the forest. The capuchin monkeys, so called because of the cowl-like arrangement of hair on the top of their heads, are the commonest of South American forms and used to be popular pets. Marmosets are also kept as pets, but these smallest of monkeys are very delicate and seldom survive long in cold parts of the world.

Old World Monkeys

The monkeys of the Old World are generally regarded as being more closely related to apes and man. They have the same number of teeth as their bigger relatives, they are less hairy than the South American forms and may have short tails, which are never prehensile. A number of species are thumbless, for the hand is used as a hook with which to hang on to branches, but where the thumb is present the hands can be used to hold and handle things as we can ourselves.

Among the common Old World monkeys are the macaques, including the rhesus monkeys of India, well known as laboratory and zoo animals. Related to them are the barbary ape of North Africa and Gibraltar and the crab-eating macaque which lives in mangrove swamps and feeds mainly on crustaceans. Also related are some small forest-dwelling African monkeys, such as the mona and the diana monkeys. Baboons are found on the ground in non-forested areas in Africa. These are extremely social animals, living in large, mobile communities. Their snout is more dog-like than in other monkeys and they are armed with large canine teeth which will be used against any attacker.

Among the monkeys with small thumbs are the beautiful colobus monkeys of Africa, and the langurs of south-east Asia, some of which are high-altitude animals. It has been suggested that the footprints of one of these may account for stories of the 'abominable snowman' of the Himalayan Mountains.

A comparison of the hands and feet of man and his primate relatives shows that man uses his hind limbs exclusively for locomotion, while most other primates use their forelimbs as well. A comparison of the hands of a tree shrew, a South American monkey and man (top to bottom) show a progression in size and flexibility.

The walking posture of monkeys, apes and man show a progressive development towards upright locomotion on two legs. Monkeys, such as baboons, which spend a good deal of their time on the ground, walk on all fours, placing the hands palms down at each stride. When walking the great apes may be capable of a few paces upright but soon drop on to their front limbs. The knuckles and backs of the fingers are used for this but never the flat of the hands. In man, a fully upright pose on two legs has been evolved.

Gibbons are very agile and move rapidly through the forests, swinging from branch to branch.

Gorilla

Apes

The true apes are all larger animals with no visible tail, and with the exception of the gibbon a rather thin coat of hair. They are all forest-dwellers, swinging through the trees by their arms, which are very long and strong. Their legs by comparison are small and weak. The hands of apes have become specialised hooks for hanging on to branches; their feet, however, have retained much flexibility and they can hold and examine objects with their big toes to a much greater extent than they can with their thumbs.

The several species of gibbon are all found in south-east Asia. They are the smallest and lightest in weight of the apes and are the most highly acrobatic, swinging and leaping at very great speed through the treetops. They are capable of running upright on the ground or along a big branch, holding their arms out to balance themselves. They are noisy, sociable animals, with few natural enemies in their forest home.

The orang-utan, which comes from Sumatra and Borneo, is by contrast a slow-moving heavyweight animal, keeping to the trees as much as possible, for it cannot move easily on the ground. Its food is mainly fruit and some invertebrates.

New World, or American, monkeys have a flat-faced look, with nostrils well separated. The Old World, or African and Asiatic, kinds have a nose in which the nostrils are close together, suggesting the prominent noses typical of human beings.

Chimps and Gorillas

Chimpanzees and gorillas are both African species. The gorilla is the largest of the apes and may weigh as much as 220 kilograms (500 pounds). Chimpanzees are much smaller, and more agile. Both travel through the forests in family parties, active during the daytime and sleeping at night in nests made in the trees of woven branches. On the ground both normally have to support themselves on their knuckles, although chimpanzees may run a few paces on their hind legs alone.

Man's close relationship with them cannot be denied, for he shares with them many bodily similarities, including the same blood group system and the fact that both can catch the same diseases. Man's treatment of his nearest relatives has been far from good, and all of the great apes are declining in numbers as a result of the destruction of their habitat. Many animals have been captured as specimens for zoos or laboratories. Conservationists hope that a complete ban may be imposed on taking these animals from their forests or we shall destroy for ever creatures that we are still far from understanding and which almost certainly have much to teach us about ourselves.

Orang-utan

Index

(A page number in bold type indicates an illustration)